Round Hall Nutcases

TORT

(Second Edition)

VAL CORBETT

ROUND HALL

THOMSON REUTERS

Published in 2009 by
Thomson Reuters (Professional) Ireland Limited
(Registered in Ireland, Company No. 80867.
Registered Office and address for service
43 Fitzwilliam Place, Dublin 2)
trading as Round Hall

Typeset by
Carrigboy Typesetting Services

Printed by
ColourBooks, Dublin

ISBN 978–1–85800–535–5

A catalogue record for this book
is available from the British Library.

Round Hall Nutcases:

TORT
(Second Edition)

In Memory of Stiofán Corbett

TABLE OF CONTENTS

PREFACE

A good knowledge and understanding of torts is one of the corner-stones of any legal education. While the word "tort" may not be instantly recognisable to the layperson, the law of torts impacts on the lives of every individual and influences human behaviour just as much as the rules of the criminal law do. Notwithstanding attacks from different sources on the current state of Irish tort law, this area of law retains a remarkable capacity to hold individuals and institutions to account for their civil wrongdoing and from preventing such wrongdoing from occurring in the first place.

The purpose of this book is to aid a student's understanding of this demanding and difficult subject. This book aims to distil the key principles and cases in the Irish law of torts into a digestible format which hopefully will provide an invaluable aid during examination revision for students as well as acting as a first point of contact for students delving into the subject for the first time.

However, nothing enhances a student's understanding of the law of torts like starting with first principles and reading the actual case law on which the majority of those legal rules and principles are based. This book is not intended to be a substitute for such learning. President Richard Nixon once said that an "iron butt" was what was necessary to make it through law school. In many ways the former President was right, nothing replaces the hours of study needed to understand and learn this complex subject. In this regard, the Irish law student is also blessed with the availability of a number of high quality treatises in this field and no personal law library should be without the works of Bryan McMahon & William Binchy, John Healy or Eoin Quill. If this book provides students with additional support or insight to these excellent texts then it will have achieved its purpose.

This book could not have been completed without the support and assistance of so many people. As any author will tell you, it is those closest to you who suffer most while you are trying to complete such a project, regardless of the size of the work. My wife, Niamh, and daughter, Jessica, deserve great credit for putting up with me throughout. I know they are both rather glad the process is now over! I also wish to thank my parents Mary and Stiofán Corbett, whose respect for education was such that I always received the fullest support during my own studies. I wish to express my gratitude to Frieda Donohue and Aisling Hanrahan at Round Hall, whose gentle guidance and superhuman patience ensured that this book was completed within a reasonable timeframe. Finally, I would like to thank all the law students whom I have taught over the past ten years or so. Whether it is at undergraduate level or on professional courses their appetite for learning and ability to ask challenging questions has ensured that my passion for this subject has never dimmed. For all my bad jokes in class, I apologise and hope I have not put you off the subject forever!

No book on torts would be complete without a disclaimer. So here it is: the author accepts no responsibility for reliance on the contents of this book and all errors are the author's own.

Val Corbett
Dublin
August 17, 2009

TABLE OF CASES

IRELAND

ENGLAND

UNITED STATES OF AMERICA

CANADA

NEW ZEALAND

AUSTRALIA

NORTHERN IRELAND

TABLE OF LEGISLATION

IRISH CONSTITUTION

IRISH LEGISLATION

ENGLISH LEGISLATION

EUROPEAN DIRECTIVES

1. NEGLIGENCE: THE DUTY OF CARE

INTRODUCTION

The law of negligence regulates careless human behaviour by providing compensation to the injured victim of another's careless conduct. The law of negligence has developed rapidly over the past century with the increase in accidents particularly since the industrialization of society.

Liability in negligence is measured primarily on the basis of *fault*. Whether the plaintiff can recover damages for the accidental injury caused by the defendant will generally depend on whether the defendant was to blame. The notion of strict (or no-fault) liability is gaining in prominence in Irish tort law and is the standard that is now imposed under the Liability for Defective Products Act 1991 and the doctrine of vicarious liability, for example. However, under the common law, fault remains the yardstick by which human behaviour is measured. Fault in this context is gauged objectively in terms of whether the defendant acted reasonably in the circumstances. Perfection is not required.

A person is guilty of negligence where he or she acts carelessly or does not take proper care in a situation where he or she should and thereby injures another party. The tort was explained thus in *Blyth v Birmingham Waterworks*:

> "Negligence is the omission to do something which a reasonable man, guided upon those considerations which ordinarily regulate the conduct of human affairs, would do, or doing something which a prudent and reasonable man would not do." (per Alderson B. in *Blyth v Birmingham Waterworks* [1856] Exch. 781 at 784)

The tort of negligence has developed in order to provide compensation to an injured party for accidental injuries he or she has suffered through the fault of another. It therefore covers a wide range of human behaviour ranging from road traffic accidents to medical mishaps. These activities are connected by a common thread, namely, the careless conduct of the defendant. In order to introduce order to the area, an overarching conceptual framework was developed which could be applied to provide a solution in any given scenario where damage has been caused by the careless conduct of another, this framework became known as the duty of care.

1

The case of *Donoghue v Stevenson* [1932] 1 A.C. 562 is considered to be the birthplace of the modern law of negligence. This case established that if the plaintiff were to succeed in an action for negligence that plaintiff needed to prove that:

1. The defendant owed the plaintiff a legal duty of care
2. The defendant breached that duty of care
3. The breach of that duty of care factually and legally caused the damage complained of, and
4. The damage was a reasonably foreseeable consequence of that breach.

The first of these questions, which is the subject of this chapter, asks whether the defendant owed the plaintiff a legal duty to take care. Before examining the duty of care principle in greater detail, it must be remembered that a finding of a duty of care is not an exact science. Essentially, when determining whether a duty of care exists in any given case, the courts must make a "value judgement" between sets of competing rights or interests. These value judgements are often disguised through the use of legal terms such as "*proximity*" and "*reasonable foreseeability*", and are also known as "*policy*". Thus while the application of the duty of care formula lends a certain coherence to the law in this area it must be remembered as Cook P. pointed out in *Mortenson v Laing* [1992] 2 N.Z.L.R. 282 that "… whatever formula be used, the outcome in a grey area case has to be determined by judicial judgement. Formulae can help to organise thinking but they cannot provide answers."

In order to properly understand the influence of policy on the duty of care formula it is necessary to follow its development in both Ireland and England since *Donoghue v Stevenson* until the present day.

THE "NEIGHBOUR" PRINCIPLE

Key Principle: A defendant will owe the plaintiff a duty of care where it was reasonably foreseeable that his or her actions or omissions would cause injury to the plaintiff (*test of foreseeability*). This duty is limited to those persons who are so closely and directly affected by the defendant's actions that they ought to reasonably have had the plaintiff in contemplation as being so affected if the defendant had properly considered the matter (*test of proximity*).

Donoghue v Stevenson [1932]

The plaintiff consumed a bottle of ginger beer purchased for her by a friend. The ginger beer was contained in a dark bottle opened on her behalf by the café owner. The plaintiff consumed some of the beer and as she poured the remainder into her glass, the remains of a decomposed snail fell out of the bottle. The plaintiff became ill and brought an action in negligence against the manufacturer of the drink. The plaintiff argued that the manufacturer of the ginger beer owed her a duty of care not to produce the beer negligently where the form in which it left the manufacturer (a dark sealed bottle) was the form it was intended to reach the ultimate consumer and in circumstances where there was no reasonable possibility of intermediate inspection which might have discovered the defect.

Held: The manufacturer was liable for the plaintiff's injury. According to Lord Atkin the defendant was under a duty not to injure his neighbour and in law, the plaintiff was considered to be the manufacturer's neighbour. This was so because it was reasonably foreseeable that should the manufacturer act negligently in producing the ginger beer such negligence would only be discovered by the ultimate consumer upon opening the bottle and consuming its contents. Notwithstanding the fact that there was no contractual relationship between the parties, the manufacturer was nevertheless found liable for the plaintiff's injuries. *Donoghue v Stevenson* [1932] A.C. 562.

Commentary

In *Donoghue*, Lord Atkin developed a generic test for the establishment of negligence. This test became known as the neighbourhood principle. Under this test, every individual owed a duty of care to his or her neighbour. A person's neighbour was identified through the test of reasonable foreseeability as limited by the concept of proximity. The test of reasonable foreseeability requires the defendant to stop and think about the predictable outcome of his or her actions. Because what is foreseeable can be almost limitless (depending on your point of view) the scope of who would fall within the duty of care would be kept in check by the additional requirement of proximity (those closely and directly affected by the defendant's actions). The test of proximity requires that there must exist some connection or relationship be it temporal, spatial, contractual or otherwise which would justify the imposition of a duty of care between the parties. A hypothetical example may best explain the distinction. Take the passer-by who witnesses a young child playing near a duck pond. It is reasonably foreseeable that this child may fall into the pond and drown. However, the law will not impose a duty of care on the passer-by. There is no legal proximate relationship between the child and the passer-by such that would impose an obligation on the passer-by to ensure that the child does not come to the perceived harm. However, if the child in question is on a school trip under the supervision of a schoolteacher, that teacher will owe a duty of care to that child in the circumstances. The danger to the child is reasonably foreseeable and there is a proximate relationship between the schoolteacher and the child i.e. the child has been entrusted to their supervision.

THE DEVELOPMENT OF THE DUTY OF CARE: *THE ENGLISH APPROACH*

Key Principle: Initially, the neighbour principle espoused by Lord Atkin in *Donoghue* was enthusiastically applied by the English judiciary.

Home Office v Dorset Yacht Co Ltd [1970]

A number of juveniles escaped from a detention centre when left unsupervised by officers. During the course of their escape, the juveniles damaged the plaintiffs' yachts. The plaintiffs argued that liability should be imposed on the Crown for the damage caused to their vessels on the basis that because the officers had failed to supervise the juveniles carefully and as they were employees of the Crown, the defendant owed a duty of care to the plaintiffs to prevent the damage from occurring.

Held: The Crown was liable for the damage caused by the juveniles. The juveniles were under the control of the officers and thus they were held responsible for their actions. As a result of their negligence (allegedly all the officers had been asleep at the time of the escape), the plaintiffs suffered foreseeable damage for which the Crown was held responsible. *Home Office v Dorset Yacht Co Ltd* [1970] A.C. 1004.

Key Principle: In an attempt to restrain what was perceived to be the overly-liberal advancement of the duty of care as exemplified by *Dorset Yacht*, a more restrictive two-stage test for establishing the existence of a duty of care was proposed by the House of Lords in *Anns* (below).

Anns v Merton London Borough Council [1978]

The plaintiff leased flats from the defendant which were structurally unsound due to a defect in the foundation. The plaintiff brought an action in negligence against the defendant Council, arguing inter alia, that it had failed in its statutory duty to inspect the foundations or had negligently carried out such an inspection thereby causing the plaintiff to suffer pure economic loss (the cost of replacing the floor).

Held: The House of Lords held that the local authority owed a duty of care to the defendant in these circumstances. In reaching this conclusion, the test for determining the existence of a duty of care was divided into two parts. First, one must ask whether there is a relationship of proximity or neighbourhood such that, in the reasonable contemplation of the former, carelessness on the part of the defendant may be likely to cause damage to the plaintiff. If it does then a prima facie duty of care was said to arise. Secondly, if the first question is answered affirmatively, it must be then considered whether there are any policy considerations which ought to negative, reduce or limit the scope of the duty. If no such considerations exist then a duty of care was said to arise. *Anns v Merton London Borough Council* [1978] A.C. 728.

Commentary

The two-stage test in *Anns* was subsequently interpreted by the English judiciary as liberalising the concept of the duty of care. According to this interpretation, the role of proximity was minimised as reasonable foreseeability was effectively equated with proximity i.e. if the damage was foreseeable then it followed that a relationship of proximity existed. At which point a prima facie duty of care could be said to arise. In practice, the courts did not tend to trouble themselves too much with the first part of the test—if the damage was foreseeable there was a tendency to hold a prima facie duty of care existed (see *Junior Books* below). In the second part of the formula, the House of Lords expressly conceded that policy did influence a finding of a duty.

As explicit policy considerations only came into consideration after a prima facie duty was held to exist this required the defendant to disprove the existence of a duty of care rather than requiring the plaintiff to prove why, based on policy, such a duty of care should be held to exist in the first place.

This interpretation of the duty of care led to what some would consider a series of increasingly liberal decisions culminating with the decision in *Junior Books v Veitchi Co Ltd* [1982] 3 All E.R. 201where a duty of care was found to exist between the defendant, was engaged to install a factory floor, and the owner of the factory, notwithstanding the fact that the installer's negligence had only caused economic loss to the plaintiff. Following this decision, a number of English decisions began to question the wisdom of adopting such an expansionist approach and the *Anns* judgment was criticised in *Governors of the Peabody Donation Fund v Sir Lindsay Parkinson & Company Ltd* [1985] A.C. 210.

Key Principle: The expansionist approach to the duty of care is no longer applied in English law. Instead, it has been replaced with a more conservative incremental case-by-case approach when assessing the existence of a duty of care in novel situations.

Caparo Industries Plc v Dickman [1990]

Caparo Industries Plc owned shares in another company called Fidelity. Caparo Industries Plc made a successful takeover bid for Fidelity after the latter's public accounts showed a £1.2 million pre-tax profit. In fact, it transpired that Fidelity had not made a profit but had made a loss of £400,000. Caparo Industries Plc brought an action against Fidelity's auditors alleging that they owed Caparo Industries Plc a duty of care which they had breached by negligently stating that Fidelity had made a profit (when they had not) and thereby causing financial loss to Caparo Industries Plc.

Held: In finding for the defendant, the House of Lords established a tripartite test for the establishment of a duty of care. The test was divided as follows: (a) was the damage foreseeable; (b) was there a relationship of proximity between the parties; and (c) was it just and reasonable to impose a duty in the circumstances.

The expansionist view adopted by English courts post-*Anns* was to be rejected and the law was to develop "incrementally by analogy with established categories". The imposition of the requirement that the court consider whether it was just and reasonable to impose a duty was designed to ensure that the court stop and think about the wider implications of finding a duty of care in the case before them. *Caparo Industries Plc v Dickman* [1990] 2 A.C. 605.

Commentary

Following the House of Lords decision in *Anns*, the English courts had adopted a liberal attitude towards the establishment of a duty of care. This relaxed approach led to a number of controversial decisions such as that in *Junior Books*. A sea-change occurred with the decisions of *Caparo* and *Murphy v Brentwood D.C.* [1990] 1 A.C. 398. In *Caparo*, the House of Lords reiterated that the tests of reasonable foreseeability and proximity were separate and distinct hurdles which needed to be individually negotiated by the plaintiff if he or she were to succeed. Crucially, *Caparo* emphasized that whether the law on negligence should be expanded into new areas depended on whether, as a matter of policy, the expansion involved a "small step" in advancing liability. This approach is known as "incrementalism" and requires that, in addition to foreseeability and proximity, the plaintiff must establish by analogy with earlier case law or precedent that the expansion of the duty of care in his or her particular case only involves an incremental development in the law (see *Sutherland Shire Council v Heyman* (1929) 60 A.L.R. 1). While incrementalism has the advantage of certainty in that the development of the duty of care is controlled to a large degree by precedent, it does sacrifice the flexibility originally envisaged by Lord Atkin in *Donoghue*. On one view, it could be said that English law replaced an overly-liberal approach (*Dorset Yacht*) with an overly-conservative approach (*Caparo*) which has hindered the development of the duty of care.

THE DEVELOPMENT OF THE DUTY OF CARE: *THE IRISH APPROACH*

Key Principle: Incrementalism did not find favour with the Irish courts and Lord Wilberforce's two-stage test as laid down in *Anns* was initially interpreted as a reiteration of Lord Atkin's neighbourhood test.

Ward v McMaster and Louth County Council [1988]

The plaintiff purchased a house from the first-named defendant with the assistance of a loan from the local County Council under the Housing Act 1966 which was designed to facilitate individuals from lower socio-economic backgrounds in purchasing their own house. Under the scheme, loan approval would be granted by the Council after the completion of an application form and following a valuation conducted by an auctioneer on behalf of the Council (for which the plaintiffs were charged a fee). After completion of the purchase the plaintiffs discovered structural defects with the house and its value was consequently greatly diminished. The plaintiffs brought an action against the Council arguing that it owed them a duty of care to carry out a proper survey of the house and that the Council's failure to do so caused foreseeable damage to the plaintiffs as it should have foreseen that the plaintiffs would have relied on the Council's valuation without conducting their own separate independent survey.

Held: The Supreme Court found in favour of the plaintiffs holding that the Council should have foreseen that—because of their limited financial means and because they had paid a fee to have the valuation carried out—they would have relied on the Council to carry out a proper survey of the property. In reaching this conclusion, McCarthy J. (with whom Finlay C.J., Griffin and Walsh JJ. concurred) approved a three-stage approach to the duty of care which provided that the duty arose because of the proximate relationship between the parties, the foreseeability of the damage, and the absence of any compelling exception based on public policy. McCarthy J. held that the proximate relationship between the Council and the plaintiffs was created by the provisions of the Housing Act 1966 which was enacted specifically to assist individuals such as the plaintiffs and that the plaintiffs' reliance on the Council's valuation was foreseeable. In his judgment, McCarthy J. appeared to specifically rejected the adoption of the incremental case-by-case approach which found favour in England post-*Caparo* observing that such an approach suffered from a temporal defect in that rights would effectively be determined by the accident of the plaintiff's birth. *Ward v McMaster* [1988] I.R. 337.

Commentary

The House of Lords decision in *Anns* was interpreted in a different manner by the Irish judiciary to that of their English counterparts. The Supreme Court in *Ward* interpreted *Anns* as a confirmation of the principles first established in *Donoghue*. This view was confirmed by Costello P. in *W v Ireland (No.2)* [1997] 2 I.R. 141. Because of the manner in which the *Anns* decision was interpreted by the Irish courts, the twin concepts of reasonable foreseeability and proximity were never merged under Irish law and thus the finding of a duty of care in novel situations never threatened to become the mere formality it had in England following *Anns*. The Supreme Court decision in *Ward* also acknowledged the importance of policy factors in determining whether a duty of care existed. McCarthy J. however did state that such factors would have to be compelling before they would prohibit the finding of a duty of care.

Key Principle: The Irish courts have now approved the incremental case-by-case approach towards the duty of care adopted by the House of Lords in *Caparo*.

Glencar Explorations v Mayo County Council [2001]

The applicant was a mining company that had been granted licenses for the County Mayo region by the Minister for Energy in 1968. The respondent introduced a mining ban as part of its development plan in 1992, despite the fact that the applicant had up to that time invested heavily in undertaking prospecting activities in the area. It was also alleged that a lucrative joint venture arrangement entered into by the applicant with another company collapsed as a direct result of the imposition of the mining ban. The applicant initiated proceedings seeking a declaration that the administrative action of introducing the ban was ultra vires, and claimed damages for negligence alleging that the Council owed a duty of care to the applicant when making its decision and had breached that duty.

Held: The Supreme Court found in favour of the respondents. Keane C.J. held that no relationship of proximity existed between the parties which would render it just and reasonable to impose liability on the respondents. On the question of the duty of care, Keane C.J. endorsed the incremental approach that had found favour in England in *Caparo*. He was of the view that no injustice would be done if, in addition to the tests of foreseeability, proximity and the absence of compelling policy factors mitigating against a finding of a duty, the plaintiff also be required to establish that it was *just and reasonable* that a finding in favour of the plaintiff should be made. This approach would ensure that novel categories of duty would only be developed incrementally by analogy with established categories in previous cases. In so doing, he appeared to sideline McCarthy J.'s pronouncements on incrementalism in *Ward* questioning whether his words on the issue actually formed part of the ratio of that judgment. *Glencar Explorations v Mayo C.C.* [2001] 1 I.L.R.M. 481 (SC).

Breslin v Corcoran & The Motor Insurers Bureau of Ireland [2003]

The defendant left his car unlocked outside a coffee shop in Dublin city centre with the keys in the ignition. A thief stole the car and had not travelled very far when he ran into the plaintiff, causing him serious injury. The plaintiff sued the first-named defendant alleging that he had been negligent in leaving the car unattended in such a manner and also joined the second-named defendant pursuant to an agreement where the MIBI had agreed to compensate the victims of uninsured driving. In the High Court, the MIBI were found wholly liable for the plaintiff's injuries. Under the agreement between the Minister for the Environment and the MIBI, the MIBI would not be held liable for the plaintiff's injuries where it was established that they were caused by the first-named defendant's negligence. Thus, in order to avoid their liability, the MIBI were obliged to argue the liability of the first-named defendant. One of the matters that fell to be decided by the Supreme Court was whether the first-named defendant owed a duty of care to the plaintiff for the thief's dangerous driving.

Held: Fennelly J. in delivering the judgment of the Supreme Court approved of Keane C.J.'s findings regarding the duty of care in *Glencar*, holding that that decision went a long way to resolving the apparent divergence which had manifested itself from the mid nineteen eighties between the approaches of the Irish courts and those of other common law jurisdictions. The court ultimately held that while it may have been foreseeable that the car would have been stolen— particularly when left unattended in such a manner on a busy city centre street—it was not foreseeable that it would have been driven in a negligent manner by the thief.

Breslin v Corcoran & The Motor Insurers Bureau of Ireland [2003] I.E.S.C. 23.

Commentary

The duty of care formula is one which is coloured by policy decisions. These policy decisions can be labelled as "foreseeability" or "proximity". At other times the court will be explicit and will state that a duty will not be imposed for "policy" reasons. However, the courts are reluctant to rely on policy alone as a reason to deny recovery to a plaintiff. As some commentators have observed, "the problem which faces the courts ... is not only to decide cases but also to justify those decisions in a way that appears rational, consistent and fair. Many judges are unwilling to fall back upon reasons of policy to justify a decision not least because such an approach indicates that a political choice is being made." (Conaghan & Mansell, *The Wrongs of Tort* (Pluto Press, 1993) at p.17). That may explain why the Supreme Court, somewhat illogically one might say, stated that the theft of the car in *Breslin* was foreseeable yet the thief's negligent driving was not.

PROXIMITY

Key Principle: Proximity is established where it is proven that there was special connection between the plaintiff and the defendant which would justify the law imposing a duty of care on the defendant. The absence of a proximate relationship will be fatal to the plaintiff's claim notwithstanding that the damage was reasonably foreseeable.

Goodwill v British Pregnancy Advisory Service [1996]

The defendant performed a vasectomy on a man who three years later became the claimant's lover. Because of his vasectomy, the claimant and the man had unprotected sexual intercourse. The claimant became pregnant and contended that the defendant owed her a duty of care and was negligent in failing to warn her lover of the possibility that he might retain his fertility.

Held: A duty of care did not exist. While the pregnancy may have been foreseeable there was no proximate relationship between the defendant and the claimant such as would justify the imposition of a duty of care. As a matter of policy, the defendant could not accept responsibility for all the women the man would have unprotected sexual intercourse with. *Goodwill v British Pregnancy Advisory Service* [1996] 1 W.L.R. 1397.

POLICY

Key Principle: While the damage may have been reasonably foreseeable and a proximate relationship may have been held to exist between the parties, the court may nevertheless refuse to impose a duty of care on the basis that it is not in the interests of policy to do so. A refusal based on policy may take into consideration, for example, issues extraneous to the parties themselves such as the fair allocation of resources or "fear of the floodgates" arguments.

Beatty v The Rent Tribunal [2006]

A landlord sought compensation from the rent tribunal arising from monetary loss suffered by him as a consequence of a decision of the tribunal regarding the fixing of rent. In the High Court, the landlord's claim in negligence succeeded and the tribunal appealed that decision to the Supreme Court.

Held: The Supreme Court agreed that the damage to the landlord was foreseeable (loss of rental income) and that there was proximity between the parties (the landlord and tenant came in direct proximity with the tribunal once it was asked to determine the rent dispute). Despite this, public policy dictated that no duty of care should be owed. The decision was justified on the basis that a public body like the rent tribunal should be free to perform its functions without the fear or threat of legal action by individuals. *Beatty v The Rent Tribunal* [2006] 1 I.L.R.M. 164.

Fletcher v Commissioner of Public Works [2003]

The plaintiff was employed as a general operative in Leinster House. One of his main duties was to assist plumbers and various tradesmen in the maintenance of the heating system in the building. The piping system was covered with a lagging containing asbestos. Through his work, the plaintiff inhaled quantities of asbestos fibres. Having been informed of the risk he was exposed to, the plaintiff was referred to a consultant respiratory physician and was told that he had not been physically injured in any way and that the chances of developing an illness as a result of his exposure was "very remote". The plaintiff was not assuaged and continued to worry that he would develop a respiratory illness. This irrational worry led to the development of a psychiatric illness known as "reactive anxiety neurosis" for which the plaintiff sought compensation.

Held: The Supreme Court was of the view that the case before them was a novel one and emphasised that policy had a role to play in the final determination. Geoghegan J. stated that the novel nature by which the injury arose required the courts to adopt a policy-centred approach to the issue. The court accepted that it was foreseeable that an individual could incur a psychiatric illness (no matter how irrationally held) in such circumstances. Further, there was no question but that a relationship of proximity existed between the employer and his employee. However, as a matter of policy Geoghegan J. found against the plaintiff on the basis that it was unreasonable, in the court's view, to impose a duty on an employer to ensure that an employee did not contract a psychiatric illness because he feared irrationally that he would contract a disease to which his or employer had negligently exposed him or her to. *Fletcher v Commissioner of Public Works* [2003] 2 I.L.R.M. 94.

Hill v Chief Constable of West Yorkshire [1989]

The plaintiff brought an action in negligence against the local police force. The plaintiff's daughter had been the final victim of the "Yorkshire Ripper", Peter Sutcliffe. The plaintiff alleged negligence against the defendants in the conduct of the investigation.
Held: The House of Lords dismissed his appeal on the basis that the imposition of liability in the circumstances would do more harm than good to society. In particular, it was feared that to impose liability on the police force in such circumstances would place an intolerable burden on public resources as the threat of litigation would distract the police force from their main duty which is the investigation of crimes. *Hill v Chief Constable of West Yorkshire* [1989] A.C. 53.

DUTY OF CARE: OMISSIONS

Key Principle: While a defendant is not normally liable for omissions, in circumstances where the defendant assumes responsibility for the plaintiff's welfare then a duty of care may arise for a failure to act.

Kent v Griffiths [2001]

The claimant's GP called an ambulance for the claimant as she was suffering from a severe asthma attack. The claimant was located

6.5 miles from the hospital, yet it took the ambulance approximately 40 minutes to arrive at the destination. The GP claimed that had she been informed that it would have taken that long for the ambulance to arrive she would have informed the claimant's husband to drive the claimant to the hospital himself.

Held: The court noted that an important feature of the case was that the ambulance was not delayed because of a lack of resources. If that were so then different considerations would come into play in determining liability. As it was, there was no good reason for the delay in the arrival of the ambulance. The acceptance of the call by the ambulance service established the duty of care. By doing so and not informing the GP of the possible delay it had voluntarily assumed the risk for the claimant's safety. *Kent v Griffiths* [2001] 2 All E.R. 474.

Barrett v Ministry for Defence **[1995]**

The deceased was a soldier on a remote base in Norway. He died while sleeping after a night of heavy drinking. Drinking in the bar on base where duty-free alcohol was available was not properly discouraged by the commanding officer. On the night of his death, the soldier had been drinking heavily and became unconscious. He was carried to his bed and left there. Sometime during the night he died due to the amount of alcohol he had consumed.

Held: The Court of Appeal found that the defendant (appellant) owed the deceased a duty of care once it assumed responsibility for his safety by putting him to bed. There was a failure to summon medical assistance and the supervision of him was inadequate. *Barrett v Ministry for Defence* [1995] 3 All E.R. 87.

DUTY OF CARE: ACTS OF THIRD PARTIES

Key Principle: Generally, a defendant is not responsible for the independent actions of third parties.

Breslin v Corcoran & The Motor Insurers Bureau of Ireland **[2003]**

The defendant left his car unlocked outside a coffee shop in Dublin city centre with the keys in the ignition. A thief stole the car and had not travelled very far when he ran into the plaintiff, causing him serious injury. The plaintiff sued the first-named defendant alleging that he had been negligent in leaving the car unattended in such a manner and also joined the second-named defendant pursuant to an agreement where the MIBI had agreed to compensate the victims of uninsured driving. In the High Court, the MIBI were found wholly liable for the plaintiff s injuries. Under the agreement between the Minister for the Environment and the MIBI, the MIBI would not be held liable for the plaintiff's injuries were it was established that they were caused by the first-named defendant's negligence. Thus, in order to avoid their liability, the MIBI were obliged to argue the liability of the first-named defendant. One of the matters that fell to be decided by the Supreme Court was whether the first-named defendant owed a duty of care for the thief's dangerous driving to the injured pedestrian.

Held: The owner of the car was not responsible for the independent negligent act of the car thief and therefore did not owe a duty of care to the injured pedestrian. *Breslin v Corcoran & The Motor Insurers Bureau of Ireland* [2003] 2 I.R. 203 (SC).

Key Principle: If there is a special relationship between the parties then a duty of care may be owed by a defendant to the plaintiff for the acts of third parties.

Dorset Yacht Co Ltd v Home Office [1970]

Borstal detainees escaped during the night when the officers in charge of them were asleep. The escapees caused damage to the plaintiffs' yachts which were moored at the nearby yacht club.

Held: Because the officers were in a position to control the young boys a duty of care was owed by the officers to the owners of the yachts. In the words of the court, "control in this context imported responsibility." *Dorset Yacht Co Ltd v Home Office* [1970] A.C. 1004.

2. NEGLIGENCE: THE STANDARD OF CARE

INTRODUCTION

A person is considered to have acted negligently where he or she fails to conform to the standard of behaviour expected by the law. The test is one of reasonableness. Did the person act reasonably in the circumstances? The standard of care is measured through the eyes of the hypothetical reasonable man. If the defendant failed to meet the standard of behaviour expected of the reasonable man in the circumstances, then he or she will be deemed to have acted negligently. The test is an objective one and as such is considered to be free of the idiosyncrasies of the particular person whose conduct is in question (*Glasgow Corporation v Muir* [1943] 132 E.R. 490). Thus, the question is not whether the defendant himself or herself acted reasonably, but whether he or she acted as the reasonable man would have done in the circumstances.

DETERMINING THE STANDARD OF CARE

In attempting to determine how the reasonable man would have acted in the circumstances, the court will have regard to the following factors:

The Probability of the Accident

Key Principle: The greater the likelihood of the accident occurring, the more likely it is that the court will find that the defendant has acted unreasonably if he or she ignores that risk.

O'Gorman v Ritz Cinema (Clonmel) Ltd [1947]

The plaintiff was sitting in the defendant's cinema. She placed her feet on the seat in front of her. The person sitting in front of the plaintiff rose from her seat and as she did so the hinge mechanism caught the plaintiff's leg. The injury to the plaintiff later turned septic. The plaintiff brought an action against the defendant in negligence.
Held: In assessing whether the defendant had acted negligently, the court took note of the fact that one million cinema goers had used the seats in the previous seven years and no similar accident had occurred.

To eradicate such accidents completely would require precautions of a fantastic nature (the removal of all the seats from the cinema). The defendant had not breached the standard of care owed to the plaintiff. *O'Gorman v Ritz Cinema (Clonmel) Ltd* [1947] I.R. Jur 35 (HC).

Bolton v Stone [1951]

The plaintiff was injured when a cricket ball hit from the defendant's ground cleared the perimeter fence and struck her while she was standing on a road outside.
Held: The defendant was not liable. It was only on rare occasions (six times in 28 years) that cricket balls cleared the perimeter of the ground and while the risk was foreseeable, the defendant was justified in ignoring it under the circumstances. *Bolton v Stone* [1951] A.C. 850.

The Gravity of the Accident

Key Principle: The defendant will be under a greater duty to reduce the risk where the consequences should it materialise are particularly severe.

Paris v Stepney B.C. [1951]

The plaintiff was blind in one eye. He worked in conditions which exposed his eyes to risk of injury, however it had been determined that these risks were not sufficient to justify the employer providing goggles to workers who were fully sighted. During the course of his work, the plaintiff was blinded by a splinter that entered his remaining good eye.
Held: The defendant was liable. The standard of care owed to the plaintiff was greater than that which would be normally owed to a fully sighted worker as the consequences of the injury occurring were particularly severe (total blindness as opposed to partial blindness). *Paris v Stepney B.C.* [1951] A.C. 367.

Vowles v Evans [2003]

The defendant was an amateur rugby referee. During a match, a front row player (who takes part in the scrummages) was injured and had to leave the field of play. At this point the referee should have asked the captain of the team whether he had an adequate replacement. If no such player was available, then under the rules the referee was required to hold uncontested scrummages for the remainder of the match. Instead, the defendant consulted with the captain who opted to replace the injured player with the plaintiff, who was a flanker, and who had no experience of playing in the front row. As a result, difficulties were encountered in the scrummage on every occasion after the injured player had departed. Eventually, one scrummage collapsed and the plaintiff was severely injured.

Held: The defendant was found guilty of negligence. He was held to have owed a duty of care to the players which he had breached by allowing the captain, contrary to the rules, to replace the injured player with the plaintiff. The standard of care expected of a referee, the court said, depended on the grade of the referee and the match he has agreed to referee. The defendant was a qualified amateur referee and he made his error during a pause in the match when he had plenty of time to decide what to do. His failure to enforce the rules in such circumstances rendered him liable. *Vowles v Evans* [2003] 1 W.L.R. 1607, C.A.

The Social Utility of the Conduct

Key Principle: If the defendant acted in a manner that was motivated by the common good, then he or she may be justified in taking what might otherwise be considered an unreasonable risk.

Hayes v Minister for Finance [2007]

The plaintiff was a pillion passenger on a motorbike which crashed while travelling at 80 miles per hour. The motorbike was being pursued by a garda car at the time of the accident. The driver of the motorbike on the night in question had failed to stop at a check point and speeded up when pursued by the gardaí. The plaintiff alleged that the gardai had breached its duty of care towards her and had caused her injuries as a result.

Held: It was legitimate for the gardaí to follow the motorbike and they had not breached the standard of care owed towards the plaintiff in the circumstances. The gardaí, while pursuing the motorbike, had modified their driving in light of the changing circumstances which occurred during the chase. In particular, the court noted that at the time of the accident the garda car had slowed down in its chase because it was aware that a road block was being prepared ahead. At the time of the crash involving the plaintiff, the garda car was stuck behind a lorry on a narrow road and was at least a mile away from the accident when it occurred. *Hayes v Minister for Finance* [2007] I.E.S.C. 8.

Watt v Hertfordshire CC [1954]

A fireman was called out on an emergency call where a woman was trapped under another vehicle. A heavy jack was needed to assist the woman. At the time of the call, there was no vehicle readily available specially equipped to carry such a jack. Rather than wait for such a vehicle to arrive, the fireman decided to load the jack onto another truck which was not suitable for such purpose. The plaintiff, another fireman, was subsequently injured when the jack rolled on the truck and injured him.

Held: The defendant was not liable. The risk of injury to the plaintiff was not so great that it should have prevented the defendant acting in the manner in which he did in order to save the woman's life. *Watt v Hertfordshire CC* [1954] 2 All E.R. 368.

Whooley v Dublin Corporation [1961]

The plaintiff injured her foot when she stepped into an open fire hydrant box on the street. The plaintiff sued the defendant in negligence. The box, which was designed to be easily accessible, had been negligently opened by vandals.

Held: The defendant was not liable. Designing the fire hydrant in a manner which would make it vandal-proof would defeat the purpose of the hydrant which was to allow for ease of access in order to assist the fire brigade. *Whooley v Dublin Corporation* [1961] I.R. 60.

The Cost of Prevention

Key Principle: The defendant may, in limited circumstances, be justified in ignoring a slight risk if the cost of remedying that risk is prohibitively expensive.

Latimer v AEC Ltd [1953]

A factory floor was flooded. The floor became very slippery as the water mixed with an oily liquid. A number of the defendant's employees were instructed to cover the floor with sawdust. Unfortunately, one part of the spillage was not cleaned up and the plaintiff slipped on the part left uncovered. The plaintiff argued that the reasonable prudent factory owner would have closed the factory down entirely until the spillage was fully cleared up.

Held: It was not necessary for the defendant to take the drastic step proposed by the plaintiff. The risk was very slight and the defendant in dealing with the risk had done everything that could be reasonably expected of him. Requiring him to close the factory down was a step too far given the nature of the risk and his initial response to it. *Latimer v AEC Ltd* [1953] 2 All E.R. 449.

Sutherland v Supervalu [1999]

A six year old girl injured her arm on a check-out conveyor belt as she was helping her mother with the groceries. The plaintiff alleged that the defendant was negligent in exposing her to such a risk.

Held: It would be unreasonable to impose a duty on shopkeepers in these circumstances. The risk which materialized in this case could only be avoided by the constant policing of young children at every check-out. Such a requirement would place an intolerable burden on the shoulders of the defendant. *Sutherland v Supervalu* (Circuit Court, March 11, 1999, *Irish Times*, March 12, 1999).

3. NEGLIGENCE: DAMAGE

INTRODUCTION

Before a plaintiff can be awarded compensation as a result of another's negligence he or she must establish that the defendant factually *and* legally caused the plaintiff's injury. While the primary purpose of tort law is to compensate the victim, it must also ensure that any compensation payable by the defendant is proportionate to his or her wrongdoing. Thus, the law has developed a two-part test for determining the defendant's liability for damage. First, the plaintiff must establish that the defendant factually caused the damage. Factual causation essentially requires the plaintiff to scientifically establish that the defendant was the cause of his or her injuries. Secondly, the plaintiff must establish that the damage suffered was a foreseeable consequence of the defendant's negligence. This determination involves questions of policy.

FACTUAL CAUSATION

1. Single Causes—*The "but for" Test*

Key Principle: If it can be established that the damage would not have occurred "but for" the defendant's negligence, then the defendant will be said to have factually caused the injury.

Barnett v Chelsea & Kensington Hospital Management Committee [1969]

The plaintiff's spouse attended the defendant's hospital complaining of severe pain and vomiting. He was not properly examined by the casualty officer on duty, and instead was advised to see his own doctor later that day. He died of arsenic poisoning soon afterwards and the plaintiff brought an action in negligence against the defendant hospital. **Held:** The defendant was not liable. Expert evidence was introduced which established that the deceased would have died from the poisoning even if he had received proper care at the defendant's hospital. In other words, it could not be said that "but for" the defendant's negligence the plaintiff's husband would have survived and therefore the defendant could not be said to be the factual cause of the death. *Barnett v Chelsea & Kensington Hospital Management Committee* [1969] 1 All E.R. 1068.

Kenny v O'Rourke [1972]

The plaintiff was a painter who was injured when he fell off a defective ladder provided to him by the defendant.

Held: Notwithstanding the defect in the ladder, the defendant was not found liable for the plaintiff's injuries. The plaintiff admitted that the reason he fell from the ladder was not because of the defect, but due to the fact that he leaned over too far while on the ladder and lost his balance. *Kenny v O'Rourke* [1972] I.R. 339 (SC).

Geoghegan v Harris [2000]

The defendant was a dentist who negligently failed to inform his patient that a dental bone graft procedure carried with it a minor risk of nerve damage. The risk materialised and the plaintiff brought an action in negligence.

Held: The defendant had acted negligently in failing to inform the plaintiff of the risks involved with the procedure. However, the defendant did not cause the harm complained of as it could not be proven that had the plaintiff been informed of the risks, he would have decided against having the procedure. *Geoghegan v Harris* [2000] 3 I.R. 536.

Commentary

The "but for" test is the test used by the courts to distinguish the irrelevant claims from those that may be relevant and can be useful as a preliminary filter. However, there still may remain a number of different possible causes of the accident and it may be scientifically impossible (in terms of the standard of proof) to distinguish one cause from the other. In recent years the courts have acknowledged that plaintiffs in such cases could be disadvantaged due to an evidentiary gap brought about by the lack of scientific knowledge available. The English courts in particular have made attempts to bridge this gap through the development of what has become known as the "material contribution" test.

2. Multiple Causation—The *"Material Contribution"* Test

Introduction

Because the material contribution test does not require the plaintiff to actually prove that the defendant caused the injuries its application is limited to specific situations involving multiple causes.

Key Principle: Where harm results from an ultimate source which is known, the defendant is found to have breached a duty of care owed to the plaintiff to prevent the particular harm from occurring and the harm which results is of a kind that the defendant was obliged to prevent, then if the breach of the duty of care *materially contributed or increased the risk of the harm occurring* the court may infer that causation has been established unless that inference is rebutted by the defendant.

Bonnington Castings v Wardlaw [1956]

The plaintiff contracted lung disease through inhaling dust in the air where he worked. The main source of this dust came from pneumatic hammers (no negligence). However, part of the dust came from the operation of grinders in the workplace (negligent). The question at issue was which dust was the source of the plaintiff's injuries. The defendant argued that there was no proof that the dust from the grinders caused the plaintiff's injuries and therefore no liability arose. **Held:** The damage arose from one ultimate known source (dust in the workplace) and the defendant's negligence could be said to be a cumulative cause. The defendant owed the plaintiff a duty of care as an employee, that duty was breached by the negligent escape of the dust from the grinders. The harm suffered by the plaintiff was of the kind which could be caused by the defendant's negligence. In such circumstances, the defendant was liable as the plaintiff was able to prove that the negligence materially contributed to the plaintiff's injuries (rather than definitively causing them) and in such circumstances the employer's negligence was held to be the sole cause of the harm. The court stated that a causative factor would be considered to have materially contributed to the damage where it was more than minimal. Where that was proven, the plaintiff was entitled to full damages for the loss suffered. *Bonnington Castings v Wardlaw* [1956] 1 All E.R. 615.

McGhee v National Coal Board [1972]

The plaintiff worked in a brick kiln. His place of work was very hot and dusty. There were no washing facilities at work and the plaintiff had to cycle home everyday covered in dust. The plaintiff contracted a skin disease. The plaintiff claimed that he would not have contracted the disease "but for" the fact that the defendant had failed to provide its employees with washing facilities. The medical evidence could not prove conclusively that the reason the plaintiff caught the disease was because there were no washing facilities nor could the plaintiff establish that the lack of cleaning facilities definitively contributed to his injuries. This was unlike the factual situation in *Bonnington* where it could be proven that the dust from the grinders contributed to the plaintiff's injury. In this case it could not be proven that the dermatitis was contracted because of the delay in washing the dust from the skin. **Held:** The House of Lords further developed the law in this area and held that, where the plaintiff can prove that the defendant's negligence had *increased the chances* of contracting the disease, the negligence could then be said to have made a *substantial contribution* to the injury. In such circumstances, the defendant would be held wholly liable for the damage on the basis that causation could be inferred. This inference would hold unless the defendant could prove otherwise. *McGhee v National Coal Board* [1972] 3 All E.R. 1008.

Commentary

The *McGhee* principle on causation benefits the plaintiff by ensuring that he or she does not suffer because of an evidentiary gap which is not of his or her making. The adoption of the material contribution test raises a number of issues. Certainly, in situations where it is impossible for a plaintiff to prove, on the balance of probabilities—because medical science may not be fully developed, for example—that one factor over all the others was the cause of the injuries, the material contribution test has the advantage of allowing the plaintiff to plug that evidential gap by requiring him or her to simply establish that the defendant's negligence materially contributed to the injury rather than having to prove that it was the sole cause. However, a danger may also exist in adopting such an approach. As Quill points out, the test, "equates risk with cause" (Quill, *Torts in Ireland*, 2nd edn, (Gill & MacMillan, 2004), at 411). In other words, a plaintiff need not prove that the defendant's actions *caused* his or her injuries, but simply that the defendant's actions *greatly increased the chances* of the injury occurring. Healy has summed up the situation as follows:

> "*McGhee* [has become] authority for the principle that the *degree* of risk created by a defendant, or the extent of his causative contribution, is no longer relevant once breach of duty and damage are together established, and that once the plaintiff establishes that the risk of injury was *greater* after the defendant's negligent act, the burden of proof of causation has provisionally been discharged and it befalls the defendant to disprove the inference that he 'caused' the plaintiff's damage." (Healy, *Principles of Irish Torts*, (Clarus Press, 2006), at 143).

Key Principle: The "material contribution" test will not be applied in circumstances where the ultimate source or agent of the plaintiff's injuries is not known and the defendant's negligence can only be considered an alternative cause of the plaintiff's injuries.

Wilsher v Essex Area Authority [1988]

The plaintiff had been born prematurely suffering from a lack of oxygen. The doctor negligently administered excessive oxygen to the child. Later, the plaintiff suffered from a number of medical complications including near-blindness. This symptom was a known complication associated with the birth of premature babies. However, it was also known that such complications could arise as a result of the negligent administration of excessive oxygen. The question before the court was whether it could be proven that the defendant's negligence was the cause of the plaintiff's injuries.

Held: In distinguishing, *McGhee* the House of Lords found that the defendant's negligence in that case exposed the plaintiff to a *cumulative* risk i.e. the dust should have been cleaned at an earlier stage. By contrast, in *Wilsher*, the defendant's negligence exposed the plaintiff to an *additional* risk which may or may not have caused the injury. Furthermore, in *McGhee*, the ultimate cause of the damage was known i.e. exposure to brick dust. In *Wilsher*, it could not be proven that the defendant's negligence greatly increased the risk of injury—it may have had nothing at all to do with the complication suffered by the plaintiff. Ultimately, the House of Lords reaffirmed the plaintiff's obligation to prove causation and found that the plaintiff had not done

so in the particular case. *Wilsher v Essex Area Authority* [1988] 1 All
E.R. 871 (HL).

LEGAL CAUSATION

Introduction

Not only must it be established that the defendant factually caused the
damage, the plaintiff must also prove that the defendant should be held
legally responsible for the harm. Thus, where an accident is caused by
a combination of an individual's negligence and natural background
conditions (e.g. speeding driver crashing on a icy road), the courts will
take the negligent act (speeding driver) rather than the background
condition (ice on the road) as being the legal cause of the accident
unless the background conditions are exceedingly abnormal (*Smith
v Leavy*, unreported, Supreme Court, November 7, 1960). Other
principles of legal causation include the *novus actus interveniens* and
the principle of remoteness of harm.

1. *Novus Actus Interveniens*

The chain of causation between the defendant's original negligence
and the plaintiff's injuries may be broken by an intervening act
unconnected to the original wrong. If this intervening act is found to
be a *novus actus interveniens*, then it will be taken to be the new cause
of the plaintiff's injuries and the defendant will be absolved of liability.
The *novus actus interveniens* may be committed by a third party, the
plaintiff himself or herself or by an intervening act of nature.

Key Principle: In order to qualify as a *novus actus interveniens*, the
intervening act must be unforeseeable.

Breslin v Corcoran & The Motor Insurers Bureau of Ireland [2003]

The first-named defendant left his car unlocked outside a coffee shop
in Dublin city centre with the keys in the ignition. A thief stole the car
and had not travelled very far when he ran into the plaintiff, causing
him serious injury. The plaintiff sued the first-named defendant
alleging that he had been negligent in leaving the car unattended. The
first-named defendant argued that the actions of the thief in stealing the

car and injuring the pedestrian by driving negligently amounted to a *novus actus interveniens* which broke the chain of causation between his negligence (in leaving the keys in the ignition) and the pedestrian's injuries (caused by the thief's negligent driving).

Held: The court rejected this line of argument. This type of thing (theft of the car) was the very thing the first-named defendant as a competent, careful and responsible driver should have guarded against. *Breslin v Corcoran & The Motor Insurers Bureau of Ireland* [2003] 2 I.R. 203 (SC).

Knightley v Johns [1982]

Having just exited a tunnel, the driver of a car negligently caused a traffic accident. The police officer in charge at the scene ordered two other police officers to go back into the tunnel in order to close the tunnel to oncoming traffic. One of these officers was injured when struck by an oncoming driver. The injured officer brought an action against his commanding officer and against the driver of the car which had caused the original accident.

Held: The arrival of the police officers following the accident was a probable and foreseeable consequence of the first driver's negligence. So too was the fact that some mistakes would be made in securing the accident scene. However, it could not have been foreseen by the driver of the car that the commanding officer would make so serious a mistake as ordering the officers into the oncoming traffic. The commanding officer's unforeseen negligent decision in sending the officers into the tunnel amounted to a *novus actus interveniens* which excused the driver from liability. *Knightley v Johns* [1982] 1 All E.R. 851.

Key Principle: The intervening act must be a voluntary one.

Conole v Redbank Oyster Co [1976]

The plaintiff sued the defendant boating company for causing the drowning of his daughter in a boating accident. The boat had been previously damaged due to the negligence of a third party and the defendant company identified the third party's negligence as a *novus actus interveniens*.

Held: The defendant's employee had taken the boat on the fateful trip when he knew that it was grounded because of the damage caused by the third party. This voluntary reckless act amounted to a *novus actus interveniens* which broke the chain of causation between the third party's negligence and the subsequent drowning. *Conole v Redbank Oyster Co* [1976] I.R. 191 (SC).

McKew v Holland & Hannon & Cubbitts [1969]

The plaintiff was injured as a result of the negligence of the defendants. His injury was slight but it impaired the proper functioning of his leg. Despite this weakness in his left leg, the plaintiff descended a steep flight of stairs which had no handrail. While descending the stairs, the plaintiff's injured leg gave way and he fell further injuring himself.
Held: The plaintiff's conduct in going down the steep flight of stairs unaided was unreasonable and had the effect of breaking the chain of causation. Lord Reid stated, "if the injured man acts unreasonably, he cannot hold the defendant liable for injury caused by his own unreasonable conduct." *McKew v Holland & Hannon & Cubbitts* [1969] 3 All E.R. 1621.

2. Remoteness of Damage

Introduction

The defendant may not be liable for all the harm that results from his or her breach of duty. In order to ensure that the defendant's liability in damages is not disproportionate to the wrong committed, the law will limit the scope of the defendant's liability to what the law deems just. Originally, the test used was that developed in *Re Polemis and Furness* [1921] 3 K.B. 560; and was known as the direct consequences test. In that case, a ship had been destroyed by fire when, due to the negligence of the stevedores, a plank fell into the hold of the ship which created a spark that ignited petrol fumes which eventually led to the destruction of the ship. The creation of the fire in this manner was deemed to be unforeseeable, yet the court found the charterers of the ship liable in negligence for all the damage. This was on the basis that, as some damage was foreseeable, the defendant should be made liable for all the damage which directly resulted. The application of the direct consequences test proved particularly severe and more often than not, the application of the test produced harsh results as the damages payable did not proportionately reflect the defendant's negligence. Thus, a new test was developed to alleviate the harshness of the rule.

Key Principle: A defendant is only liable for the foreseeable or proximate consequences of his breach of duty.

The Wagon Mound (No.1) Overseas Tankship (U.K.) Ltd v Morts Dock and Engineering [1961]

A ship was taking in oil some 600 feet away from a wharf in Sydney harbour. Due to the negligence of the charterers, some oil spilled from the ship and leaked into the harbour. Some 60 hours later, the oil had spread across the bay and was ignited due to some welding that was being carried out on the wharf. The resulting fire damaged the wharf and some ships. Applying the direct consequences test, the defendant was found liable for all the damage. The decision was appealed.

Held: The Privy Council reversed the decision of the previous court. The test as applied in *Re Polemis* was no longer considered good law. Instead, it was held that the correct test on remoteness of damage was one of reasonable foreseeability—was the damage a foreseeable consequence of the defendant's negligence? It was reasoned that to apply differing standards to determining negligence (foreseeability to the duty question and direct consequences to the damage question) was illogical. The damage was an unforeseeable consequence and the defendant was not liable. *The Wagon Mound (No.1) Overseas Tankship (U.K.) Ltd v Morts Dock and Engineering* [1961] A.C. 388.

Condon v CIE [1984]

The plaintiff worked for the defendant railway company and was suspected of being responsible for a railway accident where a number of people were killed. A tribunal of inquiry was set up by the Minister for Transport subsequent to the accident. The plaintiff was called to give evidence as a witness to the tribunal. The plaintiff brought the action against the defendant seeking inter alia damages for the costs that he had incurred as a result of appearing before the tribunal.

Held: The court adopted the *Wagon Mound* test and found that the damages sought by the plaintiff were reasonably foreseeable. In the court's view it was foreseeable that following such a tragic accident that the Minister would order an inquiry and that it was equally foreseeable that the plaintiff as an employee of the company closely involved in the incident would be called to give evidence to such a tribunal thereby incurring legal costs. *Condon v CIE* (High Court, November 16, 1984).

The Egg-Shell Skull Rule

Key Principle: If the defendant can foresee some damage resulting from his or her negligence and the plaintiff suffers greater damage than would have been reasonably expected because of some pre-existing medical condition then the defendant will be liable for all the resulting damage.

Smith v Leech Brain & Co Ltd [1962]

The plaintiff was injured at work when, due to the defendant's negligence, a piece of molten metal struck him on the lip. Due to a pre-existing condition, the burn resulted in the plaintiff developing cancer. **Held:** The defendant was liable for the cancer which developed as a result of the burn, notwithstanding that such a development had not been foreseeable. The cause of the burn should have been prevented and the fact that the extent of the damage was greater than would have been ordinarily foreseeable due to the plaintiff's medical predisposition was irrelevant. *Smith v Leech Brain & Co Ltd* [1962] 2 Q.B. 405.

Burke v John Paul & Co [1967]

The plaintiff was an employee of the defendant who was injured while cutting steel bars with a hand-operated cutter. The blades were blunt and forced the plaintiff to exert greater physical effort than should have been ordinarily required. Prior to the injury, the plaintiff had complained about the inadequate sharpness, but without response from his employer. On the day of the accident, the plaintiff suffered a hernia-related injury as a result of exerting too much pressure when using the cutter. The defendant sought a direction at the end of the plaintiff's case that it could not reasonably anticipate that the plaintiff would suffer a hernia from his work.
Held: The defendant's argument was rejected and the plaintiff succeeded in his action. It was reasonably foreseeable that the plaintiff could suffer some muscle damage as a result of using the defective equipment. The fact that the plaintiff suffered a hernia-related injury which was not foreseeable was irrelevant in the circumstances. *Burke v John Paul & Co* [1967] I.R. 277.

Key Principle: Where the plaintiff has suffered greater loss than he or she would otherwise have done due to his or her impecuniosity, he or she may not avail of the egg shell-skull rule as justification for recovery of his or her entire actual loss.

Liesboch Dredger v SS Edison [1933]

A ship owned by the defendant negligently collided with the plaintiff's ship which was carrying out dredging activities under a contract. As a result of the defendant's negligence, the plaintiff was unable to fulfil his obligations under the contract and was required to hire another dredger at an exorbitant price. The plaintiff sought recovery for the extra cost of hiring the new dredger. It transpired that it would have been cheaper for the plaintiff to purchase a new dredger outright than hiring one at such a high price, but due to cashflow difficulties the plaintiff was unable to purchase the new dredger.The defendant argued that he should only have to compensate the plaintiff in the most inexpensive manner that would right the wrong he had committed, i.e. he should only have to pay damages for the cost of purchasing a new dredger and not the hire costs incurred by the plaintiff. It was irrelevant that the plaintiff's financial situation was such that he was unable to purchase the dredger at the time.

Held: The court agreed with the defendant's argument. Lord Wright in finding that the defendant was only liable for the price of a new dredger stated that the plaintiff's impecuniosity was not traceable to the (defendant's) acts and in his opinion was outside the legal purview of the consequences of these acts. Lord Wright further stated that the operation of the egg-shell skull rule was confined to cases dealing with the extent of the plaintiff's physical damage. *Liesboch Dredger v SS Edison* [1933] A.C. 449.

4. NEGLIGENCE: DEFENCES

INTRODUCTION

There are three main defences to an action in negligence. These may be listed as follows:

1. Contributory Negligence
2. Waiver
3. Illegality

1. CONTRIBUTORY NEGLIGENCE

Introduction

The existence of contributory negligence on the part of the plaintiff acted as a complete defence to the defendant (*Butterfield v Forrester* (1809) 11 East 60). If the defendant was found to have contributed in a negligent way—no matter how slight—to his or her injuries this would act as a complete bar to recovery. However, the defence was modified and put on a statutory footing by the Civil Liability Act 1961 and its remit was extended to civil wrongs which caused injury other than negligence.

Key Principle: The defence of contributory negligence provides that where the plaintiff himself or herself has contributed to his or her injuries in some negligent way, then the damages to be awarded will be reduced by such an amount as the court deems equitable having regard to the degrees of fault of the plaintiff and defendant (s.34(1) of the Civil Liability Act 1961).

Davies v Swan Motor Co [1949]

The plaintiff's husband was killed when he was riding on the offside step of a dust-cart. It was well known that riding on the dust cart in this manner was dangerous. As the defendant's bus was overtaking the dust-cart, the plaintiff's husband was struck and killed.
Held: The defendant had acted negligently and was liable for the death. However, the award of damages was reduced in order to take

into consideration the deceased's want of care for his own safety. *Davies v Swan Motor Co* [1949] 2 K.B. 291.

Key Principle: A plaintiff is guilty of contributory negligence where he or she fails to avoid a risk of harm occurring where such harm was reasonably foreseeable.

Hussey v Twomey [2005]

The plaintiff passenger was injured in a car accident caused by the negligence of the driver of the car who was drunk.
Held: The damages awarded to the plaintiff were reduced by 40 per cent to take account of her contributory negligence in carelessly exposing herself to the danger in circumstances where that danger was foreseeable. *Hussey v Twomey* [2005] I.E.H.C. 17.

Key Principle: There must be a causal connection between the plaintiff's negligence and his or her subsequent injuries.

Jones v Livox Quarries Ltd [1952]

The defendant, contrary to known safety instructions, rode on the towbar of a vehicle while at work. He was injured when the vehicle was struck by another driven by a colleague.
Held: The award of damages was reduced due to the plaintiff's negligent behaviour in riding on the towbar which was held to have contributed to his injuries. *Jones v Livox Quarries Ltd* [1952] Q.B. 608.

2. WAIVER

Introduction

The old defence of *volenti non fit injuria* essentially provided that where an individual consented to running the risk of a particular injury he or she could not later sue because that risk materialized and caused injury. Prior to the enactment of the Civil Liability Act 1961, the plaintiff was taken to have consented where he or she was aware of the existence of the risk and yet persisted in the course of action regardless. This rule caused particular unfairness in the employment sphere as employees would be said to have "consented" to running the risk of injury simply because they continued to work in the knowledge that a danger existed. However, given the power imbalance which traditionally existed in the employment relationship could such actions be truly interpreted as consent to the risk? Under the Civil Liability Act 1961 the old defence was abolished. In order to plead the new defence it must be established that some communication between the parties took place before it can be said that the plaintiff consented to waive their legal rights in respect of the injury.

Key Principle: A plaintiff may agree to waive his or her legal rights in respect of injury, and such agreement need not form part of a legally binding contract in order to be enforceable (s.34(1)(b) of the Civil Liability Act 1961).

O'Hanlon v ESB [1969]

The plaintiff was an experienced electrician who was employed by the defendant. In order to carry out some maintenance work safely he required particular equipment which he could not access. The work could have been carried out safely if the plaintiff disconnected a nearby supply point. However, this would have disconnected the power to several houses including the one in which he was working. Alternatively, the plaintiff could have refused to carry out the work on the basis that it was too dangerous without the appropriate equipment. The plaintiff commenced the work without the necessary equipment or without disconnecting the power supply and suffered an electrical shock from an uninsulated power line.

Held: In order for the defence of waiver to operate it must be established that there was some sort of intercourse or communication between the parties from which it could be reasonably inferred that the plaintiff had assured the defendants that he waived any right of action that he might have in respect of the negligence of the defendants. There was, in Walsh J.'s view, no evidence in this particular case that the plaintiff had consented to the risk, notwithstanding that he may have been aware of the risk. As such, the court found in favour of the plaintiff and was satisfied that no such agreement existed between the parties in the present case. *O Hanlon v ESB* [1969] I.R. 75.

Key Principle: The waiver need not be expressed in writing or in another formal manner but there must be some evidence that an agreement had been reached between the parties.

McComiskey v McDermott **[1974]**

The plaintiff and defendant were occupants of a rally car which crashed during the course of a race. The plaintiff brought an action in negligence against the defendant. The defendant claimed that the plaintiff had agreed to run the risk of injury having read a sticker on the dashboard of the car which stated that "occupants travelled at their own risk".

Held: The mere presence of the sticker on the dashboard in these circumstances could not be considered an agreement between the parties for the purposes of s.34(1)(b). It transpired that the sticker had been in the car when the defendant had purchased it and the parties had joked about it and there had been no communication between the parties that the waiver represented an agreement between the plaintiff and defendant. However, the court did accept that where it is clear that such disclaimer originated with the driver and applied to the passenger, then it could be implied that a waiver had been agreed between the parties for the purposes of s.34(1)(b). *McComiskey v McDermott* [1974] I.R. 75.

3. ILLEGALITY

Introduction

This defence arises from the old common law defence of *ex turpi causa non oritur actio* (loosely translated as: no action may arise from a bad cause). This is not a defence so-called and it is more likely that the courts will refuse to hear the case if it is based on some kind of fraud, criminal activity or other immoral behavior which is deemed to be an affront to public policy.

Key Principle: It is not a defence simply to show that the plaintiff is in breach of the civil or criminal law (s.57 of the Civil Liability Act 1961).

Pitts v Hunt [1991]

The plaintiff and the deceased set off home after being on a night out. Both parties had been drinking alcohol. The plaintiff rode as pillion passenger on the deceased's motorbike. The plaintiff was aware that the deceased was not licensed or insured to drive the motorbike. The plaintiff encouraged the deceased to drive the bike in a reckless manner endangering the public and was seriously injured in an accident in which the driver of the bike was killed.

Held: The plaintiff's action failed on the grounds of public policy. The plaintiff had actively taken part and in fact encouraged the reckless driving of an uninsured, unlicensed and drunk driver. *Pitts v Hunt* [1991] 1 Q.B. 24.

Vellino v Chief Constable of Greater Manchester Police [2001]

The plaintiff failed to make a court appearance and a warrant was issued for his arrest. When the police arrived to effect the arrest the plaintiff attempted to escape by jumping from a two-storey window. The plaintiff suffered severe injuries as a result of his leap and brought an action in negligence.

Held: The plaintiff's action failed. The cause of action arose from the plaintiff's illegal act, i.e. fleeing the police, and as a result he could not succeed. *Vellino v Chief Constable of Greater Manchester Police* [2001] 1 Q.B. 24.

5. THE DUTY OF CARE: PSYCHIATRIC DAMAGE

INTRODUCTION

For the most part, the rules regarding the duty of care are well settled in cases involving physical injury. This is related, in part, to the nature of the damage. It is relatively easy to limit the scope of the duty of care owed in cases involving physical damage as that damage can be used as the anchor point in the courts' analysis. However, damage of a more intangible nature has posed greater difficulties for the courts, particularly in cases involving damage considered of a different nature e.g. cases of pure economic loss or psychiatric damage.

In cases involving damage of an intangible nature, the courts, in England in particular, have developed special rules when assessing whether a duty of care is owed in the given circumstances. In Ireland, although such cases are strictly examined, it would seem that a more principled and less categorical approach has been adopted. One of these problematical areas—and which is the subject of this chapter—is the law relating to negligently inflicted psychiatric damage otherwise commonly known as "nervous shock".

LIABILITY FOR NEGLIGENTLY INFLICTED PSYCHIATRIC DAMAGE

Introduction

Traditionally, the courts have exercised caution in awarding compensation for damage of this kind. In the English case of *Victoria Railway Commissioners v Coultas* (1888) 12 App. Cas. 222, it was held that claims for negligently inflicted psychiatric injury should not attract an award of damages. Actions for psychiatric damage, unaccompanied by any physical injury were viewed with a certain degree of skepticism by the courts. The intangible nature of such injury gave rise to fears that claims could be exaggerated or even faked. Furthermore, given the intangible nature of such damage, it was the prevailing view that to recognize such claims would open the floodgates to similar claims. However, increased awareness and understanding of the nature of psychiatric damage has led to some liberalisation of this area of law.

Development of the Tort

Key Principle: In an action for negligently inflicted psychiatric damage, a duty of care will arise where the plaintiff is in imminent danger of suffering a reasonably foreseeable physical injury.

Bell v Great Northern Railway Co [1890]

The plaintiff was a passenger on a train that became detached and rolled down a hill. While the plaintiff was not physically injured, she had suffered shock as a result of the incident and the ensuing panic it had caused. She brought an action for the distress she had suffered as a consequence.

Held: The plaintiff was successful in her action for nervous shock. The shock was the result of the physical danger she had been exposed to by the defendant's negligence and was therefore reasonably foreseeable. *Bell v Great Northern Railway Co* (1890) 26 LR (Ir) 428 (Ex Div).

Commentary

The decision in *Bell* was a reaffirmation of an earlier Irish decision in *Byrne v Southern and Western Railway Co* (1884) 26 L.R. Ir. 428 and the principle was subsequently followed in the English case of *Dulieu v White* [1901] 2 K.B. 669. While accepting the serious nature of injury of this kind, the courts did limit claims only to those who could establish that they could have suffered physical injury as a result of the defendant's negligence (i.e. were in the zone of physical danger).

Key Principle: A parent who suffers shock as a result of witnessing an incident that endangers the life of his or her child will be owed a duty of care if they have witnessed the event or its immediate aftermath, notwithstanding that they were not within the zone of foreseeable physical danger.

Hambrook v Stokes Bros [1925]

An unattended lorry rolled down a hill. The plaintiff witnessed the lorry move in the direction of her children, although she did not actually see the resulting crash. She was told that a child matching the description of her daughter had been injured. The plaintiff suffered shock as a result of the event.

Held: While the plaintiff was not in any foreseeable physical danger, the court extended liability for nervous shock to include situations where a parent was present at the scene of an accident or its immediate aftermath involving his or her child. In the view of the court this development represented a logical extension of principle. To deny recovery in such circumstances would be to ignore the strong filial bond between parent and child. This became known as the "aftermath doctrine." *Hambrook v Stokes Bros* [1925] 1 K.B. 141.

Key Principle: In aftermath situations, a defendant's duty of care to avoid causing negligently inflicted psychiatric damage may extend to include those (other than parent/child) who are in a "close relationship" with the victim.

McLoughlin v O Brian [1983]

The plaintiff's husband and children were involved in a road traffic accident. The plaintiff rushed to the hospital upon being informed of the situation. At the hospital she witnessed horrific scenes involving her family. As a result she suffered shock which led to a change in her personality. The plaintiff brought a claim for nervous shock against the defendant.

Held: The House of Lords unanimously found in favour of the plaintiff. Their Lordships differed however in the manner in which they reached their conclusions. Lord Scarman and Lord Bridge were of the opinion that the foreseeability of the damage alone should determine the issue. Lord Wilberforce and Lord Edmund-Davies on the other hand, were of the view that foreseeability was not sufficient to determine the extent of liability in such circumstances. Because of the nature of the damage, it was argued, policy or proximity factors should also be taken into consideration in reaching a decision. Motivated by a fear of the floodgates, Lord Wilberforce proposed that in addition to foreseeability of the damage, the following policy or proximity factors must be satisfied before a plaintiff could recover damages:

(1) there must be a close tie of love and affection between the plaintiff and the victim. Such a tie would be presumed in the cases of parent/child and husband/wife relationships; and

(2) the plaintiff must be close to the accident in time and space; and

(3) the plaintiff must be have directly perceived the accident with his/her own unaided senses. *McLoughlin v O Brian* [1983] A.C. 410.

Mulally v Bus Éireann [1992]

The plaintiff was informed of a road traffic accident involving her husband and children. Upon her arrival at the hospital she witnessed distressing scenes including her son covered in blood and fitted with hospital tubes. The plaintiff was severely traumatised and suffered a radical change of personality. The plaintiff claimed that the defendant owed her a duty of care not to cause her such harm in the circumstances.

Held: Denham J. in her judgment acknowledged that post-traumatic stress disorder was a recognisable psychiatric disease. In finding for the plaintiff, Denham J. applied the ordinary test of foreseeability stating that she was influenced particularly by the judgment of Lord Bridge in *McLoughlin*. In addition, she stressed that there was no policy in Irish law that prevented recovery for this type of damage in these circumstances. *Mulally v Bus Éireann* [1992] I.L.R.M. 722 (HC).

Commentary

While the ultimate outcome of *McLoughlin* and *Mulally* was identical, closer examination of the judgments display a clear divergence of approach adopted by Denham J. and Lord Wilberforce in particular. The approach of Lord Wilberforce was very restrictive. Concerned with a flood of actions, his Lordship attempted to draw a line outside of which a plaintiff could not successfully claim. In addition to foreseeability, a successful plaintiff must establish that he or she was a close relative of the victim, that he or she was close to the accident in time and space and that he or she perceived the incident or its aftermath with his or her own senses. By contrast, Denham J. appeared to adopt a more flexible approach whereby the existence of a duty would be determined primarily by the ordinary criteria of reasonable foreseeability. Policy would not play a similar arbitrary role.

The Present English Position

Key Principle: Under English law, a plaintiff who is not directly involved in the incident cannot bring an action in negligence for psychiatric damage where he or she does not satisfy the test of reasonable foreseeability and each of the policy/proximity factors outlined by Lord Wilberforce in *McLoughlin*.

Alcock v Chief Constable of South Yorkshire [1992]

A number of football fans were killed in crushing caused in a football stadium as a result of the negligence of the defendant. An action for negligently inflicted psychiatric damage was brought by a number of plaintiffs in varying degrees of relationship with the victims (including parents and brothers of the victims) but who were not present at the end of the ground where the crushing occurred. Some of the plaintiffs were situated within the ground or its immediate surroundings and some were at home at the time of the disaster. The plaintiffs' means of perception of the incident also differed. Some had witnessed the events unfold from within the stadium, others had watched television coverage of the disaster, while others had visited the makeshift morgue created in a gym where the bodies of the victims were placed for identification purposes afterwards.

Held: The defendant did not owe the plaintiffs a duty of care. Lord Keith observed that as psychiatric damage was more subtle than physical damage the ordinary test of reasonable foreseeability was not sufficient. In the view of their Lordships, the proximity limitations of relation, time, space and perception as outlined by Lord Wilberforce in *McLoughlin* were not satisfied by any of the plaintiffs. *Alcock v Chief Constable of South Yorkshire* [1992] 1 A.C. 410.

Commentary

The strict application of Lord Wilberforce's proximity limitations in *Alcock*, led to some illogical and rather harsh results. The treatment of the claims of two classes of plaintiffs is rather instructive on this point. Brian Harrison was a plaintiff present at the ground on the day of the tragedy. Mr Harrison witnessed the crushing scenes where two of his brothers died. His claim was dismissed. The fact that the victims were his brothers was not sufficient to place him within the *proximity of relationship* limitation because he had failed, in the words of Lord

Keith, to introduce any evidence of particularly close ties of love and affection with the brothers. The claims of parents who witnessed the scenes on television were also dismissed as they did not fulfil the requirement that the plaintiff perceive the incident with his or her own unaided senses. It is submitted that the tragedy and injustice visited upon the families of the victims of the Hillsborough disaster was compounded by the decision in *Alcock* which failed to apply a common sense approach towards the issue of the duty of care.

Primary and Secondary Victims

Key Principle: In English law, a distinction must be made between primary and secondary victims. A primary victim is a participant in the incident itself (the zone of danger). A secondary victim, is not directly involved in the incident (outside the zone of danger). The distinction has important practical repercussions: a primary victim must satisfy the test of foreseeability simpliciter. The secondary victim must, in addition to foreseeability, satisfy each of the proximity requirements outlined in *McLoughlin*.

Page v Smith [1996]

The plaintiff was involved in a minor road accident that was result of the defendant's negligence. Neither party was physically injured. However, the incident caused the recurrence of a mental illness in the plaintiff that he had suffered from sporadically in the past. He brought a claim in negligence for the psychiatric harm caused to him.
Held: As the plaintiff was within the range of foreseeable physical injury, he was considered to be a primary victim. In such circumstances, it was not necessary that injury of psychiatric nature be foreseeable, as foreseeability of physical injury alone was sufficient *Page v Smith* [1996] 1 A.C. 155.

Key Principle: According to English law, the primary/secondary victim classification effectively means that there is no duty on a defendant to avoid negligently inflicting psychiatric damage on bystanders or rescuers. By definition, such individuals are neither primary victims (as they are not involved in the accident) nor are they secondary victims (as they have no relationship of love and affection with the victim).

White v Chief Constable of South Yorkshire [1999]

The plaintiffs were police officers that suffered psychiatric trauma as a result of the terrible scenes that they witnessed in the aftermath of the Hillsborough football stadium disaster. The plaintiffs brought an action for negligently inflicted psychiatric damage against their employer. The plaintiffs contended that they were a special case and should be classified as primary victims for the following reasons: (a) the defendant, as their employer, owed them a special duty of care as employees; and (b) they were owed a duty of care as primary victims by virtue of their status as rescuers.

Held: The House of Lords refused to extend the duty of care for harm of this nature to the plaintiffs. They could not be categorised as primary victims and the law could not, as a matter of policy, justify such an extension. Furthermore, a finding in favour of the plaintiffs in this case would offend the ordinary public's notions of justice and fairness, when the plaintiffs in *Alcock* were denied recovery in actions which arose from the same incident. *White v Chief Constable of South Yorkshire* [1999] 2 A.C. 455.

THE PRESENT IRISH POSITION

Key Principle: To succeed in an action for negligently inflicted psychiatric damage, the plaintiff must establish that it was reasonably foreseeable that the injury arose from a shocking event and that it was reasonably foreseeable that such an event would cause him or her to suffer injury of a psychiatric nature. Furthermore, the psychiatric harm must result from the perception by the plaintiff of injury or the risk thereof being caused to oneself or another person (the shocking event). In circumstances where the plaintiff instead witnesses the aftermath of a shocking event the plaintiff must prove not only that he or she has suffered harm of a psychiatric nature, that such harm was foreseeable and that they have a close tie of love and affection with a person who was involved in the shocking event.

Kelly v Hennessy [1996]

The plaintiff's husband and daughters were involved in a road traffic accident. The plaintiff was informed of the accident via telephone. She became physically ill on hearing the news and on her arrival at the hospital became distraught at the sight of her injured family. She brought an action in negligence against the defendant.

Held: The Supreme Court found in favour of the plaintiff. Hamilton C.J. identified the following factors as ones which must be satisfied before an action could succeed:

(1)   the plaintiff must suffer from a psychiatric illness;
(2)   the illness must have been shock-induced i.e. must have arisen immediately because of the defendant's negligence;
(3)   it must have been foreseeable that the accident would cause psychiatric injury;
(4)   the illness must result from the perception of the actual injury, or a risk of injury to oneself or another person;
(5)   in aftermath situations, there must be a close personal relationship between the primary victim of the accident and the person suffering the psychiatric injury.
(6)   There was no rule of public policy to the effect that the plaintiff's claim for nervous shock, if substantiated, should be excluded. *Kelly v Hennessy* [1996] 1 I.L.R.M. 321.

Key Principle: Where the plaintiff witnesses the aftermath, the degree of relationship which must exist between the plaintiff and the victim to justify the imposition of a duty of care is not limited to parent/child or husband/wife relationships and has been extended to include siblings.

Cuddy v Mays [2003]

In that case, five people were killed when a car was rear-ended by the defendant. One of the five killed was the plaintiff's brother. The plaintiff's sister also suffered life threatening injuries as a result of the crash. All the other occupants of the car were known to the plaintiff as cousins or lifelong family friends. At the time of the accident, the plaintiff worked as a porter in the local hospital. He was on duty on the night of the accident. He recognised a number of the victims as they were brought to the hospital and was informed that one of the deceased may have been his brother. The plaintiff was then later asked by the Gardaí to identify all nine persons involved in the accident. Afterwards, the plaintiff became severely traumatised and brought an action against the defendant, the driver of the car. It was argued on behalf of the defendant that: (i) it was unforeseeable that the brother of a motorist killed in an accident would happen to be present at the nearby hospital and (ii) as a matter of policy the relationship between the plaintiff and the victims was not proximate enough (not being a relationship involving a parent/child or husband/wife) to justify the imposition of a duty of care.

Held: The High Court rejected both of the defendant's arguments. First, it pointed out that the plaintiff's claim was not based on his employment situation but primarily because of the close relationship he had with the parties and because of his physical proximity to the aftermath. Even if he had not been working that night, it was surely foreseeable that he would attend the hospital as soon as he learned of the accident. Secondly, the court noted that the previous decisions in *Kelly* and *Mulally* did not define "close family relationship" and held that in the present case the relationship of brother/sister was one which fell within the definition. Notwithstanding the finding in favour of the plaintiff, Kearns J. emphasised that policy would play a role in restricting recovery for injury of this type given the concerns which arose surrounding claims by those not actually involved in the traumatic event itself. *Cuddy v Mays* [2003] I.E.H.C. 103.

Key Principle: In this jurisdiction, the primary/secondary victim classification has not been adopted. The Irish courts instead place emphasis on the requirements of proximity, foreseeability and policy when determining liability.

Curran v Cadbury Ireland Ltd [2000]

The plaintiff turned on some machinery while at work. As a result she believed that she had killed or seriously injured another party who was working on the machine at the time. Her employer had not adopted adequate procedures in order to ensure an incident such as this would not occur. The plaintiff suffered psychiatric damage as a result of the incident.

Held: The injury suffered by the plaintiff was foreseeable and she was entitled to damages. The court noted the criticisms made by the English Law Commission of the primary/secondary victim classification which had found such favour in England and refused to adopt such an approach to the issue. Thus, notwithstanding the fact that the plaintiff was in no physical danger herself, she was entitled to recovery and it was not necessary for her to show a proximity of relationship with the individual she had injured. *Curran v Cadbury Ireland Ltd* [2000] 2 I.L.R.M. 343.

Key Principle: Notwithstanding the presence of foreseeability and proximity, claims for negligently inflicted psychiatric damage may be restricted on the grounds of policy.

Devlin v the National Maternity Hospital [2007]

The plaintiffs suffered psychiatric trauma upon learning some time after the event that their stillborn child's organs had been retained by the hospital without their knowledge or consent. The plaintiffs alleged that learning this news caused them a psychiatric trauma which gave rise to legal liability on the basis that it had been negligently inflicted. **Held:** The plaintiffs' claim failed under *Kelly* on the basis that the damage did not result from the perception of the actual injury or a risk of injury to oneself or another person. Furthermore, the plaintiffs' argument that the categories of those who could claim for such injury listed under *Kelly* should be expanded to include those such as the plaintiff was rejected by the court on the grounds of policy because any such move could, according to Denham J., give rise to "potentially unforeseeable repercussions." *Devlin v The National Maternity Hospital* [2007] I.E.S.C. 50.

6. THE DUTY OF CARE: ECONOMIC LOSS

INTRODUCTION

Pure economic loss occurs where the plaintiff suffers damage which is only financial in nature. In tort, while the courts have readily allowed recovery for economic loss which results as a consequence of physical damage, claims involving economic loss which arise independently of any physical injury have been treated with circumspection.

The distinction between pure economic loss and consequential economic loss was evident in *Spartan Steel & Alloys Ltd v Martin & Co (Contractors) Ltd* [1973] 2 Q.B. 27. In that case, due to the defendants' negligence the electricity supply to the plaintiffs' factory was unexpectedly cut off. Steel that was in the plaintiffs' furnace at the time was damaged when it solidified as a result of the power cut. The plaintiffs brought an action seeking compensation for (a) the steel that had been in the furnace at the time the power supply was cut and (b) the profits lost as a consequence of the plaintiffs being unable to produce further goods for a period of time. The court held that while the plaintiffs were entitled to compensation for the financial loss caused as a result of the damaged steel (as it was a consequence of material damage) the plaintiffs were not entitled to compensation for the loss of profits caused by the fact that the plaintiffs were unable to work as a result of the lack of a power supply (purely economic loss).

The reluctance to recognize claims of pure economic loss was motivated inter alia by the fear that by recognising such claims there would be a flood of similar claims of an indeterminate amount. Furthermore, there was a belief that such claims were more suited to the realms of contract law.

Key Principle: There is no special bar on recovery for damage of a purely economic nature. A duty of care will be established by proof of the existence of foreseeability, proximity and policy. However, given the nature of the damage, these elements may be more difficult to establish in a claim for pure economic loss.

McShane Wholesale Fruit and Vegetables Ltd v Johnston Haulage Co Ltd [1997]

The plaintiff's factory was closed because the electricity supply was cut due to a negligently caused fire on the defendant's adjoining premises. The plaintiff brought an action in negligence for the consequential loss of profits. The question of whether recovery could be obtained for pure economic loss was tried as a preliminary issue.

Held: The plaintiff's claim did not fail simply because it was of an economic nature. The issue was to be resolved based on duty of care principles as outlined by the Supreme Court in *Ward v McMaster* [1988] I.R. 337. Thus, the nature of the damage was not the dominant consideration but rather, whether the tests of foreseeability, proximity and policy were satisfied. *McShane Wholesale Fruit and Vegetables Ltd v Johnston Haulage Co Ltd* [1997] 1 I.L.R.M. 86.

Commentary

It should be noted that the judgment of Keane C.J. in *Glencar Explorations v Mayo CC* [2001] 1 I.L.R.M. 481 (SC) has cast some doubt over the broad principle expressed in *McShane*. Keane C.J.'s comments on recovery for pure economic loss had the hallmarks of the incremental approach i.e. that cases of pure economic loss would be developed on a case by case approach. Thus such claims were recognized in *Ward* (where compensation for the cost of remedying the defects in the house were recoverable against the builder and the local authority); in *Siney v Dublin Coporation* [1980] I.R. 400 (where the cost of remedying defects in a building let by the local authority were recoverable against the local authority) and in *Hedley Byrne & Co Ltd v Heller & Partners Ltd* [1964] A.C. 465 (where recovery for pure economic loss was upheld in cases of negligent misstatement). Outside of these categories Keane C.J. expressly reserved judgment as to whether recovery would be possible for such damage.

NEGLIGENT MISSTATEMENT

Key Principle: A defendant assumes a duty of care to another in circumstances where, because of a special relationship of proximity that exists between the parties, it is foreseeable that the plaintiff will rely on the safe execution of the defendant's professed skill and expertise and does so to his or her financial detriment.

Hedley Byrne & Co Ltd v Heller & Partners Ltd [1964]

The plaintiffs requested a credit reference on a potential client from its own bank. The plaintiffs' bank wrote to the prospective client's bank who replied that the client in question was in a sound financial position. The letter sent by the bank in response included the words "For your private use and without responsibility on the part of the bank or its officials." The reference was negligently prepared and the plaintiffs suffered financial loss as a result.

Held: The bank did not owe a duty of care to the plaintiffs for the negligent advice given because it contained the phrase "without responsibility". Because of the disclaimer the plaintiffs' reliance on the advice was not reasonable and no duty of care arose. However, the decision is important because the court did state that it would have found the bank liable for the pure economic loss of the plaintiffs but for the disclaimer. *Hedley Byrne & Co Ltd v Heller & Partners Ltd* [1964] A.C. 465.

Commentary

The decision in *Hedley Byrne* was an important departure by the English judiciary. Previously, pure financial loss arising from a negligent misstatement was not recoverable. Following *Hedley Byrne*, a defendant in a special relationship with the plaintiff owed him or her a duty to exercise his or her skill and knowledge in a reasonable and careful manner. The recognition of such a duty paved the way for plaintiffs in actions against other professionals, e.g. a surveyor to a mortgagee and financial institution as in *Smith v Eric S. Bush* [1990] A.C. 831; an auctioneer to clients as in *McCullagh v PB Gunne*, unreported (HC) January 17, 1997; a solicitor to a legatee (not his client) under a will as in *Wall v Hegarty* [1980] I.L.R.M. 14; and an employer in preparing a reference for an employee as in *Spring v Guardian Assurance Plc* [1995] 2 A.C. 296.

Key Principle: A special relationship of proximity must be established between the plaintiff and defendant in order to establish a duty of care for economic loss.

Caparo Industries Plc v Dickman [1990]

The plaintiffs, relying on the statutorily prepared accounts of the company, made a takeover bid for the company. The accounts had been negligently prepared and showed a profit instead of a loss. The plaintiffs sued in negligence for economic loss as they had relied on the accounts to their financial detriment.

Held: The House of Lords dismissed the action for economic loss. The accounts were prepared for a general purpose and not with the plaintiffs specifically in mind and as such a sufficient relationship of proximity did not exist between the parties. *Caparo Industries Plc v Dickman* [1990] 2 A.C. 605.

Morgan Crucible Co v Hill Samuel Bank [1991]

An accountant negligently gave advice to the plaintiff in the form of a specially prepared audit which the plaintiff relied upon to its financial detriment.

Held: The plaintiff was owed a duty of care by the defendant in the circumstances. Unlike *Caparo*, a relationship of proximity did exist. The accounts were specifically prepared with the plaintiff in mind and it was therefore readily foreseeable that it would so rely on them and where the accounts were negligently prepared it was foreseeable that they would cause economic loss to the plaintiff. *Morgan Crucible Co v Hill Samuel Bank* [1991] 1 All E.R. 142.

Key Principle: Proximity of relationship can be established where it was reasonable for the plaintiff to rely on the advice without conducting an independent enquiry.

Law Society v KPMG Peat Marwick [2000]

Solicitors' firms were under a requirement to submit accounts to the Law Society each year in order that the Law Society could, as part of its regulatory duties, confirm that the firm was in compliance with regulations on the handling of clients' money. The defendants produced such a report on behalf of a solicitor's firm but failed to notice certain irregularities with the accounts. It was subsequently discovered that the firm was involved in fraud to the tune of millions of pounds. The Law Society's compensation fund was obliged to pay out compensation to the clients of the firm who were the victims of the fraud. The Law Society brought an action against the firm of accountants on the basis that it was owed a duty of care by the firm when preparing the accounts.

Held: Based on the principles established in *Caparo*, the Court of Appeal held that in the circumstances it was readily foreseeable that the Law Society would so rely on the report produced by the accountants and that a relationship of proximity existed which justified the imposition of a duty of care in relation to such advice. *Law Society v KPMG Peat Marwick* [2000] 4 All E.R. 540.

Key Principle: It is not necessary that the plaintiff receive the advice directly from the defendant. All that is required is that the communication of that advice from the defendant to the plaintiff was reasonably foreseeable.

Wildgust v Norwich Union Life Insurance Society [2006]

The plaintiff challenged the defendant's refusal to pay out under a life insurance policy upon the death of his wife. The defendant refused to pay on the basis that the plaintiff had missed one premium payment in 1992. The failure to make payment had occurred due to a fault in the plaintiff's direct debit system. A default notice was sent to the plaintiff's insurance broker. The plaintiff and the broker had contacted the defendant a number of times in order to make the payment. The defendant confirmed to the broker that the payment had been received when in fact this had not been properly done for the purposes of the policy.

Held: The Supreme Court found in favour of the plaintiff. The defendant had negligently conveyed information to the plaintiff's broker and, while not communicated to the plaintiff himself, the defendant should have reasonably foreseen that the information would be communicated to the plaintiff and that he would rely on it. *Wildgust v Norwich Union Life Insurance Society,* SC, March 21, 2006.

Disclaimers

Key Principle: In order that it may properly insulate the defendant from liability, any disclaimer attached to the advice/information must clearly disavow liability and must be drafted carefully.

Walsh v Jones Lang LaSalle Ltd [2007]

The plaintiff purchased commercial property. The defendant auctioneer acted for the vendor during the sale. The brochure accompanying the sale of the property which had been prepared by the defendant incorrectly stated the square footage of the building. The building's size was actually 1,817 square feet less than represented in the brochure. The brochure also contained a general disclaimer which stated "whilst every care has been taken in the preparation of these particulars, and they are believed to be correct, they are not warranted and intending purchasers/lessees should satisfy themselves as to the correctness of the information given." The defendant sought to rely on the disclaimer and argued that the plaintiff should have measured the property himself. The plaintiff argued that it was common in the industry for the purchaser to rely on the brochure of a reputable firm such as the defendant's and it was not up to him to conduct his own independent measuring of the premises. It was further argued that the disclaimer properly understood applied only to minor miscalculations (which this was not).

Held: The purchaser was entitled to rely on the defendant's brochure. There was a special relationship between the parties as the brochure was directed towards the plaintiff. The disclaimer was inadequate and was not sufficient to relieve the defendant of liability. In particular, it provided that "every care had been taken in the preparation of the brochure" which it evidently had not. *Walsh v Jones Lang LaSalle Ltd* [2007] I.E.H.C. 28.

"Wrongful Life" Actions

Introduction

Claims for economic loss have also arisen in recent years in cases involving failed sterilization procedures. The question that arises before the courts in such situations is whether the law should, as a matter of policy, compensate parents for the cost of rearing a healthy, but unwanted child? Such claims were made on the basis that negligent advice on which they relied caused them to have unprotected sexual intercourse which resulted in the birth of a healthy but unexpected and unwanted child.

Key Principle: As a matter of policy, the law does not recognize a duty of care on the part of a medical practitioner who negligently advises a patient regarding the efficacy of a sterilisation procedure for the costs associated with rearing a healthy child consequently born to that patient.

Byrne v Ryan [2007]

The plaintiff had a tubal ligation at the defendant's hospital. She later became pregnant. There was some uncertainty as to whether she had been pregnant at the time she underwent the procedure or whether the procedure itself was defective. In any event, she was not informed unequivocally by the hospital that the procedure had failed. Sometime later she became pregnant with another child. It was then discovered that that the sterilisation procedure had been negligently performed. The plaintiff brought an action claiming inter alia compensation for the financial loss associated with rearing the child.

Held: The High Court refused to extend liability for such financial loss. As a matter of policy the court would not award damages to the parents for the costs of raising a healthy, but unwanted child. *Byrne v Ryan* [2007] I.E.H.C. 207.

McFarlane v Tayside Health Board [2000]

A couple agreed that they would have no more children. The husband had a vasectomy at the defendant's hospital. Afterwards, he was told to practice contraception for a while. Later, the defendant told the couple that they could now dispense with contraception as the husband's sperm count was negative. Soon after, the wife became pregnant and gave birth to a healthy child. The couple sued the defendant hospital for the pain and suffering that the wife underwent during the birth and for the costs of raising the child.

Held: The House of Lords upheld the claim for the pain and suffering caused to the wife during childbirth, but rejected the claim for the costs of raising a healthy child. While the "damage" may have been foreseeable and there was a relationship of proximity between the parties (the wife's husband was a patient of the hospital), Lord Steyn held that as a matter of policy there was no duty of care between the parties. In particular, Lord Steyn refused recovery on the basis that such an approach would not involve the fair distribution of losses, in his view, a great many ordinary people would question the fairness of awarding the parents of a healthy, but unwanted, child, damages for the costs associated with the upbringing of that child. *McFarlane v Tayside Health Board* [2000] 2 A.C. 59.

7. PROFESSIONAL NEGLIGENCE

INTRODUCTION

Professional negligence is a subset of general negligence principles. The professions which are subject to these principles have not been clearly set out, but much of the litigation in this area has related to the work of medical practitioners, solicitors and barristers.

Questions regarding the duty of care normally do not arise in cases where the negligence is alleged by a patient/client of the professional as it is readily foreseeable that the negligent work of a doctor or lawyer will cause damage to the patient or client. This chapter is primarily concerned with establishing *whether the professional exercised the appropriate standard of care*. Cases involving professional negligence differ because the holders of professional qualifications/training are to be held to a higher standard of care than that expected of the ordinary reasonable man.

MEDICAL PRACTITIONERS

Introduction

It is necessary to examine the liability of medical practitioners in relation to three particular areas of their work—diagnosis, treatment and disclosure of medical risks. The standard of care expected of the medical practitioner differs depending on whether the alleged negligence relates to his or her diagnosis and treatment of the patient on the one hand, and his or her duty to disclose medical risks associated with medical procedures on the other.

Diagnosis & Treatment

Key Principle: The standard of care expected of a medical practitioner as regards diagnosis and treatment is measured in terms of whether an individual of like specialisation and skill would have followed the same approach as the defendant had he or she been acting with the ordinary care expected of an individual of his or her experience and qualifications. This standard is measured in accordance with the General and Approved Practice ("GAP") in the profession.

Daniels v Heskin [1957]

A needle broke and became embedded inside the patient following a medical procedure. As the broken part of the needle could not be located it was left and was subsequently removed by a surgeon some weeks later.

Held: The defendant was absolved of liability in negligence. The court stated that a medical practitioner is liable in negligence for treatment of a patient if he or she does not possess the skill necessary to undertake such treatment, or if he or she does have that skill, he or she fails to exercise it with reasonable care. *Daniels v Heskin* [1957] I.R. 73.

Bolam v Friern Hospital [1957]

The plaintiff suffered fractures following electro-convulsive therapy which he had agreed to undergo as treatment for mental illness. The plaintiff alleged that the defendant had been negligent in the manner in which relaxant anesthetics had been administered and that he suffered injury as a result.

Held: McNair J. adopted a paternalistic "doctor knows best" approach. He was concerned that a pro-patient approach could be detrimental to society as a whole because it could lead to the practice of defensive medicine. The judge stated that, "a doctor is not guilty of negligence if he has acted in accordance with a practice accepted as proper by a responsible body of medical men skilled in that particular art." The treatment of the plaintiff was not negligent. *Bolam v Friern Hospital* [1957] 2 All E.R. 118.

Key Principle: The standard of care will be measured in accordance with the medical opinion of others in the profession of similar skill and qualifications. Such opinion must be derived from a respectable body of the profession.

Bolitho v City and Hackney Health Authority [1998]

A two year old patient suffered from brain damage as a result of two bouts of respiratory distress while in hospital. The doctor on call advised the nurses via telephone as to how best to treat the patient but did not attend to the patient herself. The question arose as to whether the doctor should have advised that the plaintiff be intubated after the first incident. The doctor argued that had she been present she would not have intubated the patient after the first incident. One expert testified that he would not have intubated after the first incident while five other experts testified that they would have done so.

Held: In order to assess whether the decision not to intubate was negligent the court was required to consider the opinion of suitably qualified medical practitioners. Where such expert testimony was divided the court was entitled to follow that opinion which was derived from a responsible, reasonable and respectable body of the profession. However, the court retained the discretion not to follow such evidence where it was not logically defensible. Ultimately, it was held that the decision not to intubate was not a negligent one. *Bolitho v City and Hackney Health Authority* [1998] A.C. 232.

Key Principle: Normally, adherence to a general and approved practice will relieve the medical practitioner of liability for negligence. However, if the medical practitioner follows a general practice which contains inherent defects which should have been obvious to a reasonable medical practitioner giving the matter proper consideration, then simply because that practice is used widely and over a period of time does not make that practice any the less negligent.

O'Donovan v Cork County Council [1967]

A patient was admitted to hospital operated by the defendant in order to have an appendectomy. H was the county surgeon in charge of the hospital but the patient was operated upon by the house surgeon as H was not present at the hospital at the time of the operation. When completing the procedure the house surgeon noticed bleeding which he could not stop. H was contacted and arrived to the hospital within a half hour. H assessed the patient as normal, but the patient later developed convulsions. Despite the doctor's best efforts the patient later died due to complications which arose from the procedure.

Held: H was not guilty of negligence in allowing the house surgeon perform the procedure in the circumstances. The house surgeon was well-qualified and had experience of performing such surgeries before. H had followed general approved practice in allowing the house surgeon perform the surgery. The court did qualify its finding on the basis that if the general approved practice was found to contain defects which should have been obvious to the reasonable person in the circumstances then adherence to such a practice would not necessarily absolve the practitioner of blame. As Walsh J. noted, "Neglect of duty does not cease by repetition of neglect of duty." *O'Donovan v Cork County Council* [1967] I.R. 173.

Gottstein v Maguire [2004]

The plaintiff's husband died when there was a delay in replacing a tube which was clearing the airway in his throat. The plaintiff was in hospital at the time and there was nobody qualified on duty who could have replaced the tube. The plaintiff alleged negligence against the surgeon for sending her husband to a hospital where he knew that there was nobody with the specialist training that would be needed if the tube did become displaced.

Held: While the sending of similar patients to this hospital was "common practice", the court was of the opinion that this general practice contained a defect which should have been obvious to the reasonable person had he turned his mind to it and the defendants were liable in negligence. *Gottstein v Maguire* [2004] I.E.H.C. 416.

Dunne v National Maternity Hospital [1989]

The defendant hospital had adopted a practice where in cases involving the birth of twins only the first foetal heartbeat was monitored. This was so because of the difficulty of monitoring the second heartbeat and the unreliability of any results from such monitoring. The plaintiff was severely brain damaged and his twin brother was stillborn as a result of complications which arose during birth. It was argued that had the hospital monitored both heartbeats the harm could have been avoided. The defendant appealed a jury award of IR £1,039,334 in favour of the plaintiff on the basis that the judge had misdirected the jury as to the legal principles applying to such cases.

Held: The defendant's appeal on the issue of misdirection succeeded and the damages awarded to the plaintiff were consequently reduced. The Supreme Court took the opportunity of restating the law in relation to medical negligence and summarised the position as follows:

1. Whether the medical practitioner was negligent in terms of diagnosis and treatment will depend on whether he or she has been proved to be guilty of such failure as no medical practitioner of equal specialist or general status and skill would be guilty of if acting with ordinary care.

2. If the medical practitioner deviated from a general and approved practice he or she will be guilty of negligence if it can be shown that no ordinary doctor of his or her qualifications and skill would have adopted the same route.
3. It will be no defence for the medical practitioner to say that he or she followed a general and approved practice if such GAP contained defects which should have been obvious to the ordinary reasonable doctor who gave consideration to the matter.
4. An honest difference of opinion between practitioners will not automatically lead to the assumption that the doctor is guilty of negligence in taking one view over another.
5. It is not for the court to decide which form of treatment was preferable that should be judged in accordance with the view of similarly qualified and experienced practitioners.

Dunne v National Maternity Hospital [1989] I.R. 91.

Key Principle: It is not for the court to decide which form of treatment is preferable when assessing negligence.

Shuitt v Mylotte [2006]

The defendant carried out a radical hysterectomy on the plaintiff. He based his decision on the fact that a CT scan showed signs of malignant disease. No report written or verbal on the CT scan was produced prior to surgery which indicated the existence of a tumor. Nevertheless the defendant informed the plaintiff that he believed such a tumor existed and he immediately prescribed the surgery. The plaintiff alleged that the defendant should not have operated without first having received a written report. It was also alleged that he should have conducted other scans prior to advising in favour of the surgery.
Held: The court approved the *Dunne* principles. It noted that it was not its function to decide which course of treatment was preferable, but whether it could be proven that the defendant was guilty of such negligence as no other similar doctor would be guilty of. As there was conflicting testimony as to the correct course of treatment which should have been undertaken, the plaintiff had not established that the defendant had been negligent and was guilty of a practice that no other reasonable medical practitioner would have followed. *Shuitt v Mylotte* [2006] I.E.H.C. 89.

Key Principle: While the court will respect the profession's view as to which method of treatment is preferable, it will not allow the profession to usurp the courts' role as the ultimate arbiter of the issue in circumstances where the experts agree on the preferred method of treatment.

Griffin v Patton [2004]

The doctors had failed to retrieve some bone when performing an operation on the plaintiff's womb. In the High Court, the medical experts from both sides agreed that the correct procedure had been carried out, however they disagreed as to whether the surgery had been negligently performed or not.

Held: The Supreme Court found that the "honest difference of opinion" rule in *Dunne* applied to differences regarding diagnosis and ways of treating a patient. Where the correct procedure to be carried out was agreed upon, then there is nothing to prevent the court from deciding the issue of fact as to whether that procedure was correctly carried out or not. *Griffin v Patton,* Supreme Court, July 27, 2004.

DISCLOSURE OF MATERIAL RISKS

Introduction

The doctrine of informed consent provides that a medical practitioner is under a duty to disclose all known material risks with a particular treatment to the patient in order that the patient may make a fully informed decision as to whether it will proceed with the treatment. The leading case in this area is the Canadian decision of *Canterbury v Spence* (1972) 464 F 2d 772. In that case, a 19 year old plaintiff signed a consent form on the basis that it was no more serious than any other operation. The operation led to the plaintiff's partial paralysis. The plaintiff argued that the defendant had been negligent in not disclosing the one per cent risk of paralysis associated with the procedure. The defendant stated that it was not proper to disclose such risks to patients, arguing that it would scare patients off from undertaking necessary operations and the question was one which ultimately had to be decided by the medical practitioner. The court rejected the defendant's claim and found that such cases were properly to be assessed under negligence principles and not under trespass to the person. Regarding the standard of care to be applied, the court stated that disclosure was not to be assessed in accordance with GAP as very little consensus exists amongst the medical community as to the kinds of risks that should be revealed to a patient. Crucially, the court determined that respect for the patient's right to self determination meant that the standard of care in relation to disclosure should be one imposed by law rather than one imposed by the medical profession upon themselves.

Key Principle: In cases of elective surgery, a medical practitioner is obliged to disclose risks, however exceptional or remote, of grave consequences involving severe pain for a period of time into the future.

Walsh v Family Planning Services Ltd [1992]

In that case, the plaintiff underwent a vasectomy. He suffered an adverse reaction and was in severe pain afterwards. He claimed inter alia that the risks associated with the procedure had not been properly explained to him.

Held: Finlay C.J. appeared to favour an application of the *Dunne* test to the question of disclosure while O'Flaherty J., in cases of elective surgery at least, appeared to favour a materiality test—if there was a risk of grave consequences involving severe pain into the future, then the medical practitioner was under a duty to disclose. *Walsh v Family Planning Services Ltd* [1992] 1 I.R. 496.

Key Principle: A medical practitioner is under a duty to disclose all material risks associated with a particular form of treatment. Whether a risk is material will depend on the severity of the consequences should the risk materialise, the statistical frequency of the risk occurring and the circumstances under which the patient presented himself or herself for treatment.

Geoghegan v Harris [2000]

The plaintiff had a dental procedure which involved taking a bone graft from his chin. He began to suffer severe pain after the operation. He claimed that he had not been informed of the risks which were possible (less than one per cent chance of paralysis) and was simply told that it was no more risky than other medical procedures.

Held: Kearns J. found himself bound by one element of *Walsh* which provided that where the treatment is elective the defendant must disclose all known risks, however remote, of grave consequences or severe pain associated with the treatment. Kearns J. applied a reasonable patient standard similar to that adopted in *Canterbury* and held that the defendant should have disclosed the risk to the plaintiff. *Geoghegan v Harris* [2000] 3 I.R. 536 (HC).

Key Principle: A warning must now be given in every case where there is a significant risk associated with the treatment which would affect the judgment of a reasonable patient. Furthermore, a late warning communicated to the patient may be deemed inadequate for the purposes of informed consent.

Fitzpatrick v White [2007]

The plaintiff had a squint since birth. He underwent corrective surgery which greatly improved it. In 1993, he decided, for cosmetic reasons, to undergo further surgery to correct the squint. The surgeon warned the plaintiff a half hour before the operation—while he was sitting in his hospital gown waiting for the procedure—that there were some risks associated with the surgery. The surgery was carried out properly with no evidence of negligence, but unfortunately due to a rare anomaly the patient was left in a worse condition that he had been in before he had agreed to the surgery. The patient suffered from double-vision and headaches as a consequence.

Held: The plaintiff had been warned of the risks associated with the procedure. Notwithstanding the fact that the warning had been delivered at a late stage prior to the procedure the Supreme Court held that in the circumstances it was adequate. The Supreme reaffirmed the decision of the High Court in *Geoghegan*. *Fitzpatrick v White* [2007] I.E.S.C. 51.

Key Principle: The plaintiff must prove that the negligent failure to warn caused the plaintiff's injuries.

Geoghegan v Harris [2000]

The plaintiff had a dental procedure which involved taking a bone graft from his chin. He began to suffer severe pain after the operation. He claimed that he had not been informed of the risks which were possible and was simply told that it was no more risky than other medical procedures and that had he been so informed he would have decided against undergoing the procedure.

Held: While the defendant's failure to warn was negligent, the plaintiff could not prove that had he been warned he would have decided against having the treatment thereby avoiding the outcome. *Geoghegan v Harris* [2000] 3 I.R. 536 (HC).

Chester v Afshar [2004]

The plaintiff suffered from chronic pain over a six year period. At one stage she was reduced to sitting in a wheelchair from the pain. Conservative treatment proved ineffectual. The plaintiff was referred to a consultant who recommended surgery which she was reluctant to undergo. After some dispute it was accepted that the defendant had failed to warn the plaintiff of a small (1 per cent to 2 per cent) but unavoidable risk that the proposed operation, however expertly performed, might lead to a seriously adverse outcome. The plaintiff underwent the surgery and the random risk materialized and she was paralysed as a result.

Held: The surgery had not been negligently carried out but the defendant was negligent in failing to warn the plaintiff of the risks in circumstances where he should have. While it could not be said that had she been warned of the risks she would never have undergone the surgery, the plaintiff's argument was that as a matter of policy a medical practitioner should be held liable for damage caused by a materialized risk which he had foreseen and where he failed to warn the patient of that danger. In this case, under the "but for" test the plaintiff was unable to establish that she never would have undergone the surgery—thereby failing on straightforward principles of causation. However, the House of Lords did accept that had she been informed of the risk (as she should have been) then she would have decided not to undergo the surgery at that time and would have sought a second opinion before then undergoing the surgery. Thus, she was deprived of the opportunity of having the surgery at a different time and because the chances of "lightning striking twice" were extremely remote it was unlikely that the risk would have materialized on the second date allowing her to avoid the outcome. The defendant was liable. *Chester v Afshar* [2004] U.K.H.L. 41.

Commentary

The reasoning of the decision in *Chester* clearly does not accord with normal causation principles and some might say that the plaintiff's line of argument is far-fetched. Establishing causation in cases of informed consent can be particularly problematical. In cases such as these, one is dealing with "the patient's hindsight and bitterness" and it will usually be the case that a patient, who has not been informed of all material risks and is then injured by the occurrence of that risk, will argue that things would have been different if only he or she had been informed of the risk before consenting to the treatment. In many ways, it is easy to say that *after* the event and therefore in order to ensure that the profession is not placed under intolerable pressure, the courts have demanded that the plaintiff prove *objectively*—using the "but for" test—that he or she would not have undergone the procedure had he or she known of the risk prior to the treatment. On the other hand, one must consider whether, as a matter of policy, a medical practitioner who is aware of a serious risk should always be liable for failing to disclose the possibility of such a risk occurring in circumstances where that risk does subsequently materialize. In other words, can the patient's right to self-determination be truly protected unless the failure to disclose is itself actionable?

SOLICITORS

Key Principle: The standard of care expected of a solicitor is similar to the standard set out for medical practitioners in *Dunne v National Maternity Hospital*. Thus, a client is entitled to the degree of care and skill expected of a reasonably careful and skilful solicitor.

Roche v Peilow [1986]

The plaintiff purchased property from a building company. The defendant—who was acting for the plaintiff in the transaction—failed to make a simple search of the Companies Register to ascertain whether any charges had been created over the property by the defendant company. Such searches were not standard practice by solicitors. The plaintiff suffered a loss when it was subsequently discovered that the property was subject to a charge in favour of a bank.

Held: The solicitor was found liable in negligence. The solicitor had mindlessly and automatically followed a practice of others when, if he had taken the time to think about it, he would have recognized the dangers for his client of continuing to follow such an approach. *Roche v Peilow* [1986] I.R. 232.

Edward Wong Finance Co Ltd v Johnson [1984]

The defendant solicitors, following a practice amongst the profession in Hong Kong, paid the purchase price to the vendors in return for the promise to ensure that the property was free from encumbrances. The vendors fraudulently gave such assurance as a result of which the plaintiffs did not obtain unencumbered title to the property.

Held: While the evidence was that this practice was universally adopted in the profession, this was not sufficient for the solicitors to avoid negligence. The risk should have been foreseen and the defendant should have taken steps to avoid it. *Edward Wong Finance Co Ltd v Johnson* [1984] A.C. 296.

Key Principle: A solicitor not only has a duty of care to his or her clients but may also owe a duty of care to third parties.

Wall v Hegarty [1980]

A solicitor negligently failed to ensure that a will had been properly attested by two witnesses. As a result, a beneficiary under the will was denied a legacy worth a significant financial sum.

Held: The intentions of the testator were not to be frustrated by the negligence of the solicitor who was found to owe a duty of care to all beneficiaries under the will. *Wall v Hegarty* [1980] I.L.R.M. 124 (HC).

Key Principle: A solicitor owes a duty of care when advising clients. However, this duty does not extend to requiring the solicitor to provide unsolicited advice to the client.

Rojack v Taylor and Buchalter [2005]

The plaintiff engaged the defendant solicitors to administer her mother's estate. The plaintiff later claimed that the defendant should have advised her that she could maintain a claim against the estate on the basis that it did not make proper provision for her.

Held: No such duty could be expected of the defendant. They had been engaged to administer the estate and had done so. *Rojack v Taylor and Buchalter* [2005] I.E.H.C. 28.

BARRISTERS

Key Principle: Barristers no longer enjoy immunity from suit in respect of their preparatory work or their management of the trial itself.

Behan v McGinley **[2008]**

The plaintiff alleged that his then barrister (now deceased) had failed to secure for him adequate financial compensation in earlier proceedings as a result of his negligent management of the case. He alleged inter alia that the barrister had not produced certain documents before the court and had not aggressively cross-examined certain witnesses.

Held: While the plaintiff's claims were ultimately dismissed on the facts, the court did state that barristers no longer enjoyed a blanket immunity from suit for their negligent behaviour in such circumstances. *Behan v McGinley* [2008] I.E.H.C. 18.

8. DEFAMATION

INTRODUCTION

The right to freedom of expression and the right to a good name are constitutional rights which will, at times, collide. It is the function of the courts, through the tort of defamation, to ensure that the proper balance is struck between these competing rights. The tort recognizes that freedom of expression is to be protected but its exercise should not come unjustly at the expense of another's reputation.

It is the right of every citizen to freely express his or her opinions. Such a right is sacrosanct in any democratic society and is guaranteed under Art.40.6.1 of the Constitution. However, the right to freedom of expression is not unlimited and is subject to some qualification, otherwise it would be open to abuse. Thus, the application of Art.40.6.1 may be restricted by Art.40.3.2 of the Constitution which guarantees that the State, by its laws, protects from unjust attack or, in the case of injustice done, vindicates the good name of every citizen.

This area of law was reformed with the enactment of the Defamation Act 2009. In this chapter the relevant statutory provisions are included alongside the previous position at common law. Where the common law and statutory position under the 2009 Act conflict it will be the statutory position which shall apply to future cases which fall within its jurisdiction.

ELEMENTS OF THE CAUSE OF ACTION

Definition at Common Law

Defamation is the wrongful publication of a false statement which tends to lower that person in the eyes of right thinking members of society or tends to hold them up to hatred, ridicule or contempt or causes them to be shunned by right thinking members of society. (per Walsh J., *Quigley v Creation Ltd* [1971] I.R. 269.)

Definition under the Defamation Act 2009

Section 6(2) states that: "The tort of defamation consists of the publication, by any means, of a defamatory statement concerning a person to one or more than one person (other than the first-mentioned person), and "defamation" shall be construed accordingly."

1. Publication

Key Principle: The false statement must be communicated to a third party. Publication can take many forms, all that is required is that the information is wrongfully conveyed to a third party. Section 6(1) of the 2009 Act has now abolished the distinction between libel and slander. Instead, they shall be collectively described as the "tort of defamation."

Youssoupoff v Metro-Goldwyn-Mayer Pictures Ltd [1934]

The plaintiff brought an action in libel against the defendant regarding a motion picture which suggested that she had been raped by the monk, Rasputin.
Held: The film was libellous. The film was found to be a permanent form of publication. *Youssoupoff v Metro-Goldwyn-Mayer Pictures Ltd* (1934) 50 T.L.R. 581.

Monson v Tussauds Ltd [1894]

The plaintiff was charged with murder in Scotland where a verdict of not proven was returned. The defendant produced a waxwork model of the plaintiff and placed it in its Chamber of Horrors. The plaintiff brought an action in libel.
Held: It was held that the presentation of the waxworks model in these circumstances amounted to a publication and was libellous. *Monson v Tussauds Ltd* [1894] 1 Q.B. 671.

Key Principle: The general principle is that every publication of a defamatory statement can amount to a fresh cause of action. Therefore, the defendant may be liable in defamation where he or she has republished a defamatory statement originally made by another person.

Berry v Irish Times Ltd [1973]

The defendant reproduced a photograph of a picketer holding a placard in protest, which accused the plaintiff of assisting the British government to jail terrorists. The plaintiff alleged that this statement was defamatory.

Held: The defendant had published the statement for the purposes of defamation by reproducing the photograph in this manner. *Berry v Irish Times Ltd* [1973] I.R. 368.

Key Principle: Section 6(4) of the 2009 Act provides that publication for the purposes of the tort does not occur where the statement is published to a person to whom it relates or to another person where:
(a) it was not intended that the statement would be so published to that other person, and
(b) it was not reasonably foreseen that publication to the first named person would result in the statement being published to the other person.

Paul v Holt **[1935]**

A letter the defendant wrote was addressed to a Mr Paul and sent it to his home. The plaintiff's brother happened to live at the same address and opened the letter. He then showed it to his wife and to the plaintiff's wife. **Held:** The defendant was found to have published a defamatory statement even if it was accidental. Evidence was introduced which showed that the defendant was aware that the plaintiff's brother lived at the same address. The publication was foreseeable and as such was liable in defamation. *Paul v Holt* (1935) 69 I.L.T.R. 157.

2. Defamatory Statement

Key Principle: The statement must be capable of damaging the reputation of another. The test as to whether a statement is defamatory is an objective one i.e. does it lower the individual in the eyes of *right thinking* members of society. (per Walsh J. in *Quigley v Creation Ltd* [1971] I.R. 269).

Section 2 of the 2009 Act defines a defamatory statement as: "a statement that tends to injure a person's reputation in the eyes of reasonable members of society."

Berry v Irish Times Ltd **[1973]**

A statement contained on a placard read "Peter Berry 20th Century Felon Setter – Helped jail Republicans in England." The statement referred to the plaintiff who was the Secretary to the Department of Justice at the time. The plaintiff alleged that as the words implied that he was an informer, they were defamatory if untrue.

Held: Notwithstanding the negative connotation that such an accusation may have historically in Ireland, it was not defamatory. The statement—viewed objectively—accused the plaintiff of informing the authorities of illegal terrorist activities. Such an accusation could not therefore be deemed to be defamatory. *Berry v Irish Times Ltd* [1973] I.R. 368.

Byrne v Deane [1937]

A golf club was raided by the police acting on the information of an informant. Illegal gambling machines were seized during the raid. Afterwards a verse was posted on the clubhouse wall stating "but he who gave the game away, may he byrne in hell and rue the day." The plaintiff brought an action in libel on the basis that the words were defamatory as they implied that he was a disloyal person.
Held: There was no defamation. Looking at the words objectively, the plaintiff's reputation could not be tarnished by a statement which implied that he had informed the police of certain illegal activity. *Byrne v Deane* [1937] 1 K.B. 818.

Key Principle: Whether a statement is defamatory is a question of fact and not law. The statement should be examined in light of the words said, the person concerned and the general circumstances surrounding the publication. Any words and gestures used will be given their ordinary and natural meaning.

Reynolds v Malocco, t/a Patrick [1999]

The plaintiff was a well-known Dublin nightclub owner. He brought an action against the defendant regarding a magazine article referring to him as a gay bachelor. The defendant contended that the word "gay" was an adjective used to describe the plaintiff's joyful and "happy go lucky" nature and was not intended as commentary on his sexuality.
Held: The words used should be given their ordinary meaning and in the judgment of the court they were being used to describe the plaintiff's sexuality in this case. In the words of Kelly J. "one would have to be a resident on the moon not to be aware of the fact that the word was synonymous with homosexuals and homosexual activity." The statement therefore implied that the plaintiff was a hypocrite who was concealing his true sexuality from the public. *Reynolds v Malocco, t/a Patrick* [1999] 1 I.L.R.M. 289.

Key Principle: An innuendo may give rise to an action in defamation. The innuendo arises where a statement is made which appears innocent on its face but where a secondary defamatory meaning may be implied from the publication by "reading between the lines" (false innuendo) or because of certain extrinsic facts which are independently known by the reader (true innuendo) and of which the publisher is aware.

Campbell v Irish Press Ltd [1955]

The plaintiff was involved in the business of supplying snooker equipment. He organised an exhibition match involving a famous snooker player. In a review published by the defendant the next day it was stated that the snooker player had not achieved a maximum break because "the table told lies" i.e. that the table was defective in some way.

Held: The court accepted the plaintiff's argument that the statement was capable of being defamatory. The implication of the words was that the equipment provided by the plaintiff was faulty and that he was incompetent in his organisation of the exhibition. *Campbell v Irish Press Ltd* (1955) 90 I.L.T.R. 105 (SC).

Tolley v Fry & Sons Ltd [1931]

The defendant published a cartoon featuring the plaintiff, a famous amateur golfer, promoting Fry's chocolates. The plaintiff claimed that the publication of the cartoon implied that he had consented to his image being used in such a manner which he had not. He argued that the publication of the cartoon was defamatory as he was an amateur golfer and it implied that he was receiving financial reward and was therefore prostituting his amateur status.

Held: The cartoon and its accompanying caption wrongly implied that the plaintiff had agreed to promote the defendant's product for financial reward which would be in direct contravention of his amateur status and was defamatory of him. *Tolley v Fry & Sons Ltd* [1931] A.C. 333.

Cassidy v Daily Mirror Newspapers Ltd [1929]

The defendant published a photograph of the plaintiff's husband (Mr Cassidy) with another woman. The accompanying caption stated that

Mr Cassidy had recently become engaged to the woman. The plaintiff brought an action in defamation.

Held: The publication of the photograph was defamatory of the plaintiff. It implied that she had not been married to Mr Cassidy and had been living immorally with him. *Cassidy v Daily Mirror Newspapers Ltd* [1929] 2 K.B. 331.

Lewis v Daily Telegraph [1964]

The defendant newspaper published a story which was headed "Inquiry on firm by City Police." The story alleged that the fraud squad were inquiring into the affairs of a company, of which the claimant was chairman. The claimant alleged that the story implied that the affairs of the company were being carried out dishonestly.

Held: The words could not be interpreted as meaning that the company was involved in fraud. The story merely stated that the company was the subject of an inquiry. *Lewis v Daily Telegraph* [1964] A.C. 234.

Commentary

The statement must be capable of damaging the plaintiff's reputation. It is clear that the courts will take into consideration the context in which the statement was made (*Reynolds v Malocco*). The statement need not imply dishonesty or incompetence in order to be considered defamatory. If it tends to hold the plaintiff up to hatred ridicule or contempt, it may be actionable. Thus, in *Berkoff v Burchill* [1996] 4 All E.R. 1008, the defendant's description of the actor, Stephen Berkoff, as being "hideously ugly", was capable of being defamatory. Furthermore, mere words of vulgar abuse will not be defamatory. In *Hoebergen v Koppens* [1974] 2 N.Z.L.R. 597, calling somebody a "Dutch bastard" was not actionable, as it was not intended to be descriptive of the defendant's character.

Section 9 of the Defamation Act 2009 provides that a person can only bring one cause of action for defamation in respect of the publication of a defamatory statement even if the more than one defamatory imputation lies within the published statement.

Key Principle: A misleading defamatory impression contained within a publication will only give rise to an action in defamation if the reasonable reader, having viewed the publication in its entirety, would consider that it was defamatory of the plaintiff. For example, a potentially defamatory newspaper headline could be neutralised if the accompanying article corrects the misleading impression. This is known as "the bane and antidote" test.

McGarth v Independent Newspapers [2004]

The defendant published a photograph of the plaintiff, a CIE worker, by way of a correction of an early publication error, with a caption entitled "businessman ... who borrowed to invest €9,600 in Eircom shares, not €50,000 as reported." The photograph appeared under the headline of an entirely unrelated article headlined "Big Business linked to Family of Terrorist." That story dealt with the links between Osama bin Laden and certain companies. The plaintiff argued that, due to the positioning of the article and the photograph, the implication was that he was linked to terrorism.

Held: Gilligan J. accepted the "bane and antidote" test and held that in order for a claim in defamation to exist, "the headline, the article, the accompanying photograph and caption underneath the photograph have to be considered in their totality" and furthermore the meaning that such a publication, in its totality, would convey to the ordinary fair minded reader. It was held that the totality of the publication in question was not capable of conveying to the ordinary fair minded reader a meaning that the plaintiff was linked to terrorists. *McGarth v Independent Newspapers,* unreported, High Court, Gilligan J., April 21, 2004.

Charleston v News Group Newspapers Ltd [1995]

The plaintiffs were actors who played Harold and Madge in the TV soap, *Neighbours.* They brought an action in defamation against the defendant because of the publication of an article which contained the headline "Strewth! What's Harold up to with our Madge?" Beneath the article was a photograph of two naked people engaged in explicit sexual activity. There was also a smaller photograph in a similar vein with the plaintiffs' heads superimposed on the bodies of porn actors. The article went on to refer to a pornographic computer game which superimposed the actors' heads onto the bodies of others without their consent.

Held: The article taken as a whole was not defamatory of the plaintiffs. The House of Lords found that one cannot take isolated parts of a story (such as the headline) without considering the full context. The test to be applied as to the meaning of the publication would include, "the meaning, including an inferential meaning, which the word would convey to the mind of the ordinary, reasonable, fair-minded reader." Thus notwithstanding the shock headline and the danger that certain readers would simply glance at it without reading through it fully, the test had to be of the ordinary reader (akin to the reasonable man in negligence) who read the article in its entirety and gleaned the full meaning. *Charleston v News Group Newspapers Ltd* [1995] 2 A.C. 65 (HL).

3. Identification of the Plaintiff

Key Principle: The plaintiff must establish that the defamatory statement identifies him or her. Section 6(3) of the 2009 Act provides that "a defamatory statement concerns a person if it could reasonably be understood as referring to him or her."

Sinclair v Gogarty [1937]

The defendant in his book, made a defamatory reference to "two Jews on Sackville Street." The plaintiff brought an action in defamation alleging that the defendant had been referring to him.
Held: The ordinary reader of the book would understand that the statement referred to the plaintiff and could give rise to an action in defamation. *Sinclair v Gogarty* [1937] I.R. 377.

Key Principle: Whether the defendant intended to refer to the plaintiff in the publication is irrelevant.

E. Hulton & Co v Jones [1910]

The defendant published a fictional newspaper article regarding a one Artemus Jones. The article accused Mr Jones of immoral behaviour. The real Mr Jones, who was a practising barrister, brought an action in defamation alleging that the article referred to him and was defamatory.
Held: The defendant argued that the fact that the plaintiff shared a similar name to the individual in the article was merely coincidential. However, the court found in favour of the plaintiff, the motivation of the defendant in publishing the material is irrelevant and if the ordinary general public upon reading the statement, honestly and reasonably believe that the article referred to the plaintiff, then it will be considered defamatory and an action will exist. *E. Hulton & Co v Jones* [1910] A.C. 20.

Key Principle: Whether an individual member of a group can bring a claim for defamation where the group is defamed will depend on whether a reasonable person would identify the individual as being so affected.

Section 10 of the 2009 Act now provides that a member of a class of persons shall have an action in defamation where:

> "(a) by reason of the number of persons who are members of that class, or
>
> (b) by virtue of the circumstances in which the statement is published, the statement could reasonably be understood to refer, in particular, to the member concerned."

Le Fanu v Malcolmson [1848]

An article about the cruelties performed by Irish factory owners was not defamatory as it was deemed to be too general to have specifically identified the plaintiff. However, the article proffered further information in relation to the plaintiff's factory in Waterford city.
Held: This additional information was sufficient to allow the plaintiff to ground an action as he was sufficiently identifiable from that additional information. *Le Fanu v Malcolmson* (1848) 9 E.R. 408.

Key Principle: The position of the individual within the group could be determinative as to whether that individual has been identified.

Orme v Associated Newspapers [1987]

A potentially defamatory article was published regarding the activities of a religious cult known as the Moonies.
Held: The article directly impugned the reputation of the leader of the cult as it implied that as leader of the group he was aware of the activities alleged to have occurred within the group. *Orme v Associated Newspapers, The Times,* December 10, 1987.

DEFENCES TO AN ACTION IN DEFAMATION

Introduction

The tort of defamation itself seeks to vindicate the constitutional right each citizen has in his or her own name. The defences which are available to an action in defamation are designed to vindicate the defendant's right to freedom of expression. In addition to creating new defences, the 2009 Act has made significant modifications to the defences which already existed at common law. Following the enactment of the Defamation Act 2009 the following are the defences which are now available to a defendant in an action for defamation:

1. Truth
2. Absolute privilege
3. Qualified privilege
4. Fair and reasonable publication on a matter of public interest
5. Honest opinion
6. Offer to make amends
7. Apology
8. Consent
9. Innocent Publication

In this section of the chapter, the statutory defence will be discussed followed by a description of the position which existed at common law prior to the introduction of the 2009 Act.

1. Truth

Key Principle: Section 16 of the 2009 Act provides that it will be a defence to an action for defamation for the defendant to prove that the statement was "true in all material respects." Where the statement contains two or more allegations, the defence of truth will not fail, "if the words not proved to be true do not materially injure the plaintiff's reputation having regard to the truth of the remaining allegations."

Alexander v North Eastern Railway Co **[1865]**

The plaintiff was charged with travelling on a train without paying the appropriate fare or having the correct ticket. The plaintiff was fined and sentenced to two weeks' imprisonment. The defendant published a poster that stated that the plaintiff had been fined and was sentenced to three weeks' imprisonment. The plaintiff brought an action in defamation due to the inaccuracy in the statement.
Held: The defendant successfully pleaded the defence of justification. While the statement may have contained some factual errors, the part

that was not true did not alter the general tenor of the statement, i.e. that the plaintiff had been convicted of travelling without the correct ticket. *Alexander v North Eastern Railway Co* (1865) B. & S. 340, 122 E.R. 1221.

Cooper-Flynn v RTÉ [2000]

It was alleged in a television programme that the plaintiff had encouraged clients to purchase investment portfolios for the purpose of evading tax. In the programme, the third-named defendant alleged that he had been personally encouraged by the plaintiff to invest in such a scheme. The plaintiff brought an action in defamation and the defendants argued that the defence of justification applied.
Held: While the jury found the allegations of the third-named defendant to be untrue, they held that, in the context of the programme as a whole, the plaintiff had indeed encouraged others to take part in such a scheme. The defence of justification succeeded. *Cooper-Flynn v RTÉ* [2000] I.R. 344.

Key Principle: The defence must prove that the "sting" of the defamation is true.

Grobbelaar v News Group Newspapers Ltd [2002]

The plaintiff was a famous professional footballer. The defendants published a series of articles alleging the plaintiff had dishonestly taken bribes, had fixed or attempted to fix the result of games of football in which he had played and that he had taken bribes with a view to fixing the result of games in which he would be playing in. The allegations were based on video recordings made of the plaintiff in conversation with another individual where he discussed receiving such payments and discussed fixing the results in games. The plaintiff argued that he had never thrown football games for money and that the recorded conversations were just a ploy by the plaintiff to discover who was behind the match-fixing attempt. In action for defamation, the plaintiff was awarded damages of £85,000 by a jury. The defendants appealed the verdict of the jury as perverse and the award was successfully overturned by the Court of Appeal. The plaintiff appealed to the House of Lords.
Held: The finding at first instance that the defendants were liable was not a perverse finding by the jury. One interpretation of the jury's

finding was that the sting of the libel by the defendants lay in the fact not that the plaintiff accepted corrupt payments but that he did so to throw football matches. On that basis, the defendants were obliged to prove the truth of the sting in the libel i.e. that he accepted payment to fix matches. In relation to this part of the story, the defendants had claimed that the plaintiff had deliberately let in a goal in one particular game. However, evidence from the plaintiff (including expert testimony from a former professional goalkeeper) was to the effect that he had not done so. The defence of justification therefore failed. However, the award of damages was reduced to £1. *Grobbelaar v News Group Newspapers Ltd* [2002] U.K.H.L. 40.

2. Absolute Privilege

Absolute privilege arises where the law considers that the public interest is best served by guaranteeing uninhibited expression in particular contexts. This is an absolute privilege in the sense that it protects all statements made, howsoever motivated, in the relevant context.

Section 17 of the 2009 Act lists the following as occasions of absolute privilege and includes statements:

"(a) made in either House of the Oireachtas by a member of either House of the Oireachtas,

(b) contained in a report of a statement, to which paragraph (a) applies, produced by or on the authority of either such House,

(c) made in the European Parliament by a member of that Parliament,

(d) contained in a report of a statement, to which paragraph (c) applies, produced by or on the authority of the European Parliament,

(e) contained in a judgment of a court established by law in the State,

(f) made by a judge, or other person, performing a judicial function,

(g) made by a party, witness, legal representative or juror in the course of proceedings presided over by a judge, or other person, performing a judicial function,

(h) made in the course of proceedings involving the exercise of limited functions and powers of a judicial nature in accordance with Article 37 of the Constitution, where the statement is connected with those proceedings,

(i) a fair and accurate report of proceedings publicly heard before, or decision made public by, any court—

  (i) established by law in the State, or

  (ii) established under the law of Northern Ireland

(j) a fair an accurate report of proceedings to which a relevant enactment referred to in section 40 of the Civil Liability Act 2004 applies,

(k) a fair and accurate report of proceedings publicly heard before, or decision made public by, any court or arbitral tribunal established by an international agreement to which the State is a party including the Court of Justice of the European Communities, the Court of First Instance of the European Communities, the European Court of Human Rights and the International Court of Justice,

(l) made in proceedings before a committee appointed by either House of the Oireachtas or jointly by both Houses of the Oireachtas,

(m) made in proceedings before a committee of the European Parliament,

(n) made in the course of proceedings before a tribunal established under the Tribunals of Inquiry (Evidence) Acts 1921 to 2004, where the statement is connected with those proceedings,

(o) contained in a report of any such tribunal,

(p) made in the course of proceedings before a commission of investigation established under the Commissions of Investigation Act 2004, where the statement is connected with those proceedings,

(q) contained in a report of any such commission,

(r) made in the course of an inquest by a coroner or contained in a decision made or verdict given at or during such inquest,

(s) made in the course of an inquiry conducted on the authority of a Minister of the Government, the Government, the Oireachtas, either House of the Oireachtas or a court established by law in the State,

(t) made in the course of an inquiry conducted in Northern Ireland on the authority of a person or body corresponding to a person or body referred to in paragraph (s),

(u) contained in a report of an inquiry referred to in paragraph (s) or (t),

(v) made in the course of proceedings before an arbitral tribunal where the statement is connected with those proceedings,

(w) made pursuant to an in accordance with an order of a court established by law in the State."

3. Qualified Privilege

Key Principle: Section 18(2) of the 2009 Act provides that the defendant can avail of the defence of qualified privileged where it can be proved that:

"(a) the statement was published to a person or persons who—
  (i) had a duty to receive, or interest in receiving, the information contained in the statement, or
  (ii) the defendant believed upon reasonable grounds that the said person or persons had such a duty or interest, and
(b) the defendant had a corresponding duty to communicate, or interest in communicating, the information to such person or persons."

Qualified Privilege at Common Law

Key Principle: Notwithstanding their defamatory content, certain statements will be protected on occasions where one party has a *duty to speak* or is under an *obligation to protect an interest,* and the recipient has a corresponding interest in receiving the information.

"Duty"

Kirkwood Hackett v Tierney **[1952]**

The President of UCD, in the presence of the College Secretary, wrongly questioned a student about a money draft that had been paid out in error.
Held: The court found that the communications between the College President and the student were privileged. The President had a duty to make such an enquiry of the student in the presence of the College Secretary. *Kirkwood Hackett v Tierney* [1952] I.R. 185.

Kearns & Co v the General Council of the Bar **[2002]**

The Bar Council received a letter of complaint from a barrister. He was concerned about instructions that junior barristers were receiving from a firm known as Kearns Agency and believed that this firm had breached the Bar's code of conduct. Having reviewed the matter, the Bar Council forwarded a circular to all chambers and senior clerks to the effect that Kearns & Co was not a firm of solicitors and that it would be improper for barristers to receive instructions from Kearns

Agency. It transpired that the Bar Council were incorrect, Kearns & Co were indeed a firm of solicitors and Kearns Agency was a body recognised by the Law Society and was entitled to instruct counsel.

Held: The defendant successfully pleaded the defence of qualified privilege. The Bar Council had a duty to deliver this information to its members, and in the absence of malice on their part, the information was considered privileged. *Kearns & Co v The General Council of the Bar* [2002] 4 All E.R. 1075.

"*Interest*"

Key Principle: A statement made in order to protect an interest may be subject to qualified privilege.

McCormack v Olsthoorn [2004]

The plaintiff, a retired Garda Superintendant, had gone shopping in an outdoor market. He was searching for specific types of tomato plant. He purchased one type and was examining another at the defendant's stall. He put the plant back down and continued walking while holding the original plant that he had purchased elsewhere. The defendant saw the plaintiff walking away with what he thought was his property and approached the plaintiff asking him if he had taken his plant and could he return to the stall with him. The plaintiff alleged that the allegations made against him were defamatory and were particularly damaging because he was well known in the area as a former Garda Superintendent and a regular customer at the market. The defendant argued that he was entitled to act in a non-malicious way in order to protect his property.

Held: The statement was protected by qualified privilege. It did not matter whether the accusation was reasonable as long as it was not made with malice it was protected. *McCormack v Olsthoorn* 1 I.E.H.C. 431.

Note: The statutory definition of qualified privilege under the 2009 Act now requires that the defendant's belief must be on reasonable grounds.

"*Malice*"

Key Principle: Where the information is communicated for an improper purpose or motive then the privilege will be lost. A statement is motivated by malice in circumstances where the maker of the statement did not honestly believe that what he or she stated was true or was reckless as to whether it was true or not.

Horrocks v Lowe [1975]

During a council meeting, the defendant councillor accused the plaintiff councillor of misleading the finance committee of the council in relation to a dispute between Bolton Corporation and a company of which the plaintiff was chairman. The defendant sought the plaintiff's removal from the council because he was of the view that the plaintiff's many property interests would lead to potential conflicts of interest. The plaintiff brought an action in slander against the defendant. While he did accept that the occasion during which the statement was made was privileged, the plaintiff argued that the privilege had been destroyed by the defendant's malice.

Held: In order to defeat the defence of qualified privilege, the plaintiff must establish that the defendant's dominant motive for making the statement was not to protect the relevant interest or perform the relevant duty, but arose from personal spite or other bad motives. The House of Lords found that in this instance, there was no evidence that the defendant had acted out of a predominantly malicious motive and that he honestly believed in the truth of the statement he had made, as such, the statements were privileged. *Horrocks v Lowe* [1975] A.C. 135.

Berber v Dunnes Stores Ltd [2006]

A manager employed by the defendant had circulated a duty roster to management personnel under the heading "new trainees" which included the plaintiff's name. The plaintiff had worked for 21 years with the defendant and had only been recently moved to store management. The plaintiff contended that this description of him was defamatory.

Held: The court accepted that the publication of the duty roster was an occasion governed by qualified privilege and that there was no evidence of ill intent on the part of the manager when he included the plaintiff's name on the list. *Berber v Dunnes Stores Ltd* [2006] I.E.H.C. 327.

4. Fair and reasonable publication on a matter of public interest

Key Principle: Section 26 of the Defamation Act 2009 created a new defence of fair and reasonable publication. This defence will apply if the defendant can prove that:

"(a) the statement in respect of which the action was brought was
       published—
       (i)   in good faith, and
       (ii) in the course of, or for the purpose of, the discussion of a
             subject of public interest, the discussion of which was for
             the public benefit,
 (b) in all of the circumstances of the case, the manner and extent of
       the publication of the statement did not exceed that which was
       reasonably sufficient, and
 (c) in all of the circumstances of the case, it was fair and reason-
       able to publish the statement."

Matters which the court shall take into consideration when assessing whether the publication was fair and reasonable

Section 26(2) provides that the court shall take into consideration such
matters as it thinks relevant when considering whether the publication
was fair and reasonable, including any or all of the following:

"(a) the extent to which the statement concerned refers to the
       performance by the person of his or her public functions;
 (b) the seriousness of any allegations made in the statement;
 (c) the context and content (including the language used) of the
       statement;
 (d) the extent to which the statement drew a distinction between
       suspicions, allegations and facts;
 (e) the extent to which there were exceptional circumstances that
       necessitated the publication of the statement on the date of
       publication;
 (f) in the case of a statement published in a periodical by a person
       who, at the time of publication, was a member of the Press
       Council, the extent to which the person adhered to the code of
       standards of the Press Council and abided by determinations of
       the Press Ombudsman and determinations of the Press Council;
 (g) in the case of a statement published in a periodical by a person
       who, at the time of publication, was not a member of the Press
       Council, the extent to which the publisher of the periodical
       adhered to standards equivalent to the standards specified in
       paragraph (f);

(h) the extent to which the plaintiff's version of events was represented in the publication concerned and given the same or similar prominence as was given to the statement concerned;

(i) if the plaintiff's version of events was not so represented, the extent to which a reasonable attempt was made by the publisher to obtain and publish a response from that person; and

(j) the attempts made, and the means used, by the defendant to verify the assertions and allegations concerning the plaintiff in the statement."

Furthermore, s.26(3) provides that where the defendant fails to obtain the plaintiff's version of events either because the plaintiff refuses to respond or fails to respond, then such a lack of response shall not imply that the plaintiff has consented to the publication of the statement nor is a court entitled to draw any inference therefrom.

Qualified Privilege and the Media at Common Law

Key Principle: Media defendants may plead a special form of qualified privilege when publishing information which is deemed to be in the public interest, provided that the publication is of a particular quality.

Reynolds v Times Newspapers Ltd **[1999]**

The defendants published a story about the plaintiff the former Taoiseach of Ireland which was entitled "Goodbye Gombeen man". The general tenor of the story was that the plaintiff had deliberately and dishonestly misled the Dáil. The defendants claimed that the story should be covered by a generic qualified privilege related to political information. They argued that they were under a duty to publish the information and that the general public had a corresponding interest in receiving the information concerning as it did, an Irish politician who was well-known to the British public through his work with the peace process in Northern Ireland.

Held: The House of Lords rejected the argument that political information such as that contained in the offending article should be covered by a generic qualified privilege. Lord Nicholls was of the view that the introduction of such a concept would not provide adequate protection for the reputation of the individual. Their Lordships were also concerned that the defence would be extended to public figures other than politicians which would create its own difficulties. Finally, the House was of the view that proof of malice would not be sufficient to protect an individual's reputation in this situation highlighting the fact that under English law, a newspaper is not obliged to divulge its sources. Such a rule would make it incredibly difficult for the plaintiff to prove malice. Their Lordships did however accept that under certain circumstances the defence could succeed where the following "shopping list" of ten factors were satisfactorily considered:

(1) The seriousness of the allegation.
(2) The nature of the information and extent to which it is a matter for public concern.
(3) The source of the information.
(4) The steps taken to verify the information.
(5) The status of the information.
(6) The urgency of the matter.
(7) Whether the defendant sought comment from the plaintiff.
(8) Whether the article contained the gist of the story.
(9) The tone of the article.
(10) The circumstances of publication.

In the present case it was held that the defendant could not rely on the defence as it had failed—in the English version of the paper—to print the plaintiff's side of the story. *Reynolds* v *Times Newspapers Ltd* [1999] 1 All E.R. 609.

Grobbelaar v News Group Newspapers Ltd [2001]

The Court of Appeal held that the defence of qualified privilege was not successfully pleaded. In that case the plaintiff was a famous professional footballer. The defendants published a series of articles alleging that the plaintiff had taken bribes in order to fix football matches. The allegations were based on a video tape sting arranged by the defendants where it was alleged that the plaintiff had admitted to the offences.
Held: The defence of qualified privilege did not succeed as a defence. Utilising the ten-steps devised by Lord Nicholls in *Reynolds*, the court held that the articles were not occasions which should be protected by qualified privilege. In particular, it was the court's view that the exposé did not contain the plaintiff's side of the story and that the timing and

tone of the article were designed to suit the defendant's interests. *Grobbelaar v News Group Newspapers Ltd* [2001] 2 All E.R. 437.

Jameel v Wall Street Journal (Europe) [2004]

The plaintiffs in this case were a Saudi businessman and the trading company of which he was president and general manager. The defendant published an article asserting that, at the request of US enforcement agencies, the Central Bank of Saudi Arabia was monitoring certain bank accounts to prevent their use in the channeling of funds to a number of terrorist organizations. The plaintiff's trading company was listed as an account holder. The plaintiff sued in defamation as the article was inaccurate and the defendant pleaded *Reynolds'* privilege. At first instance the defence failed because the defendant had failed to obtain the plaintiff's response to the story prior to publication.

Held: On appeal the decision was overturned by the House of Lords and the defence of qualified privilege succeeded. Lord Hoffman was critical of the negative manner in which *Reynolds* had been applied by courts up to that point. He was of view that the shopping list in *Reynolds* was to be applied holistically and not as separate distinct hurdles. The shopping list were simply factors which would assist a court in determining whether the "duty/interest" test was satisfied and were not to be used as barriers to raising the defence. *Jameel v Wall Street Journal (Europe)* [2004] U.K.H.L. 44.

The Public Interest Defence at Common Law

Key Principle: A media defendant may have a defence to an action for defamation where it can be established that the publication was in the public interest and that the steps taken to gather and publish the information were responsible and fair.

Leech v Independent Newspapers (Ireland) Ltd [2007]

The plaintiff sued the defendant newspaper following the publication of an article which reported on an incident which has occurred on live national radio the day before. The newspaper article recounted how the radio show unexpectedly broadcast an allegation of improper conduct between the plaintiff and a government minister which allegedly would have explained why the plaintiff had been paid for certain work by the government. The High Court was asked to rule, whether a defence of public interest could be raised in the context of the case and be put before the jury in the trial.

Held: In determining that it could, Charleton J. found that a defence of public interest suffered by association with traditional qualified privilege. He suggested that malice under that defence be replaced by an examination of the professional conduct of journalists under the defence of public interest. This defence would arise where:

(a) the subject matter of a publication, considered as a whole, was a matter of public interest; and

(b) once a public interest is established, then it must be considered whether the steps taken to gather and publish the information were responsible and fair.

In considering whether the steps taken to gather and publish the information were responsible and fair, the court was entitled to take into consideration the shopping list of factors listed in *Reynolds*. On the facts of the case itself, the court found that the defence could not be put to the jury. While both parties accepted that what was broadcast on radio was unacceptable, there was a genuine public interest in publishing information to the public regarding the failure of the national public broadcaster to take steps (a 20 second delay, for example) to prevent such occurrences on live radio. The court found in particular that the fact that the journalist who wrote the article did not appear in court to defend his actions was strong evidence that the second part of the test had not been made out. It was decided that the defence would not be put to the jury for deliberation. *Leech v Independent Newspapers (Ireland) Ltd* [2007] I.E.H.C. 223.

Commentary

Section 26 of the 2009 Act replaces the common law public interest defence with one of "fair and reasonable publication on a matter of public interest." The defence is actually much stricter than that provided by the *Leech* decision and will not be easy for a defendant to establish. In order for the defence to apply it must be made in *good faith* and during the course of or for the purpose of *public discussion* which was for the *public benefit* and that it was *fair* and *reasonable* in all the circumstances to publish the statement. Furthermore, the Act gives further weight to the Press Council as the court may take into consideration the extent to which the defendant adhered to the code of standards of the Press Council (where the defendant is a member of the Press Council).

5. Honest Opinion

Key Principle: Section 20 provides for the defence of honest opinion which replaces the common law defence of fair comment. The defence provides that where the statement consists of opinion, that opinion must be honestly held. Section 20(2) provides that an opinion is honestly held if:

"(a) at the time of the publication of the statement, the defendant believed in the truth of the opinion or, where the defendant is not the author of the opinion, believed that the author believed it to be true,

(b) (i) the opinion was based on allegations of fact-

(I) specified in the statement containing the opinion, or

(II) referred to in that statement, that were known, or might reasonably be expected to have been known, by the persons to whom the statement was published,

or

(ii) the opinion was based on allegations of fact to which-

(I) the defence of absolute privilege, or

(II) the defence of qualified privilege,

would apply if a defamation action were brought in respect of such allegations,

and

(c) the opinion related to a matter of public interest."

Section 21 provides guidance on how a court shall distinguish between allegations of fact and statements of opinion. Such analysis shall have regard to the following:

"(a) the extent to which the statement is capable of being proved;

(b) the extent to which the statement was made in circumstances in which it was likely to have been reasonably understood as a statement of opinion rather than a statement consisting of an allegation of fact; and

(c) the words used in the statement and the extent to which the statement was subject to a qualification or a disclaimer or was accompanied by cautionary words."

Fair Comment on Matters of Public Interest at Common Law

Key Principle: Honestly expressed opinions on matters of public interest which are based on facts or privileged communications, shall be protected by the defence of fair comment.

Convery v The Irish News Ltd [2008]

Two journalists wrote a less than complimentary review of the plaintiff's restaurant. Some of the statements in the article referred to the fact that the cola they were served was "warm and watery" and "must have come from a tap." The review also stated that the larger choice on the menu "makes it impossible to use fresh food unless you're prepared to spend a lot of money on staff." The review also noted that the squid must have been made from "reconstituted fish meat … and cannot have been real squid." Furthermore, the review observed that the "chicken Marsala" was inedible. The plaintiff brought an action in defamation.

Held: The plaintiff succeeded at first instance but the decision was overturned on appeal on the basis that the trial judge had misdirected the jury regarding the distinction between factual statements made (not protected by fair comment) and simple commentary or opinion (which was protected by fair comment). The court held that statements such as the "cola was warm and watery" and the "chicken Marsala was inedible" were plainly comments and not statements of verifiable fact. *Convery v The Irish News Ltd* [2008] N.I.C.A. 14.

Key Principle: The comment must relate to a matter of public interest for the defence to apply.

London Artists Ltd v Littler [1969]

A number of actors in a play terminated their contracts through their agents, the plaintiffs. The defendant producer alleged that the plaintiffs and the actors had colluded to end the play. The plaintiffs brought an action in defamation and the defendant contended that the defence of fair comment protected his statement.

Held: The Court of Appeal reiterated that the comments must be made on a matter of public interest before the defence of fair comment could apply. In this context, the public interest was interpreted widely to include comments made on the operation of government, literature and the arts. Further, the comment must be based on matters of established fact. In this case, the defendant's plea of fair comment was ultimately unsuccessful as he failed to establish as a fact that there had been a plot between the actors and the plaintiffs. *London Artists Ltd v Littler* [1969] 2 Q.B. 375.

Commentary

The distinction between comment and fact lies at the heart of this defence. If a statement of fact is published it cannot be protected by the defence of fair comment and will only be protected if defamatory where it is proven to be true or is privileged. The distinction between comment and fact was summed up neatly by Ferguson J. in *Myerson v Smith's Weekly* (1923) 24 S.R. (NW) 20 at 26, when he stated, "To say a man's conduct was dishonourable is not comment, it is a statement of fact. To say that he did certain specific things and that his conduct was dishonourable is a statement of fact coupled with a comment." The commentary must, either expressly or implicitly, refer to the factual matrix on which it is based in order that the reader himself or herself can make a judgment as to whether the comment is well founded. Commentary tends to involve criticism, conclusions, deductions or observations on certain facts. Finally, the commentary must be related to the factual matrix on which it is based i.e. criticizing an artist's style or work when reviewing a play would be fair comment, but questioning the artist's morality would not—*Merivale v Carson* (1887) 20 Q.B.D. 275.

6. Offer to make amends

Key Principle: Section 22 provides that a person who publishes a defamatory statement can make an offer to make amends. This offer should be in writing, state that it is an offer to make amends in accordance with the Act and must state whether the offer is in respect of the entire statement or refers only to part of the statement or a particular defamatory meaning within it. An offer to make amends means an offer:

(a) to make a suitable apology or correction regarding the statement

(b) to publish that apology or correction in a manner which is reasonable and practicable

(c) to pay to the person any compensation or damages or costs as agreed by the parties.

7. Apology

Key Principle: Section 24 provides that where the defendant has made or offered an apology to the plaintiff in respect of the defamatory statement and has published (or offered to publish) that apology in such a manner so that the apology was given the same or similar prominence as was given to the original statement, it will be evidence in mitigation of damage. Critically, s.24(3) provides that an apology made by or on behalf of the defendant no longer constitutes an express or implied admission of liability by the defendant nor is it relevant to the determination of liability and is not admissible in any civil proceedings as evidence of the liability of the defendant.

8. Consent

Key Principle: Section 25 provides that it is a defence for a person to prove that the plaintiff consented to the publication of the statement.

9. Innocent Publication

Key Principle: Section 27 provides that it shall be a defence for the defendant to prove that:

"(a) he or she was not the author, editor or publisher of the statement to which the action relates,

(b) he or she took reasonable care in relation to its publication, and

(c) he or she did not know, and had not reason to believe, that what he or she did caused or contributed to the publication of a statement that would give rise to a cause of action in defamation."

Section 27(2) provides that a person is not an author/editor/publisher of a statement if:

"(a) in relation to printed material containing the statement, he or she was responsible for the printing, production, distribution or selling only of the printed material,

(b) in relation to a film or sound recording containing the statement, her or she was responsible for the processing, copying, distribution, exhibition or selling only of the film or sound recording,

(c) in relation to any electronic medium on which the statement is recorded or stored, he or she was responsible for the processing, copying, distribution or selling only of the electronic medium or was responsible for the operation or provision only of any equipment, system or services by means of which the statement would be capable of being retrieved, copied, distributed or made available."

Godfrey v Demon Internet [2001]

The defendant Internet Service Provider (ISP) hosted a website where an unknown person posted material which indicated that the material had been posted by the claimant. The posting was a forgery and was defamatory of the claimant. The claimant sent a fax to the defendant on January 17 informing the defendant of the posting and requesting that it be removed immediately. The post was not removed and expired naturally on January 27.

Held: The defendant was liable for the losses which arose from January 17 until the expiration of the posting on January 27. Up until that point the defendant had only played a passive role in the publication. However, once the defendant had been informed of the defamatory material it was under an obligation to take reasonable steps to deal with the posting which it had failed to do. *Godfrey v Demon Internet* [2001] Q.B. 201.

9. OCCUPIERS' LIABILITY

INTRODUCTION

This area of law governs the duties, liabilities and rights which are attached to occupiers' in respect of dangers to entrants due to the condition of the occupied property. In other words, it concerns the duties owed to persons who enter onto another's property in respect of dangers upon that property. Thus, it only relates to injuries caused to such entrants which arise due to the *state of the premises*, rather than the actions of any individual on such premises.

Historically, the law favoured the occupier of property over the entrant. The courts very much adopted an attitude of *laissez faire* (non-interference)—it was up to the entrant to look out for himself or herself. The level of duty owed by an occupier to an entrant depended very much on the type of entrant—the greater the benefit conferred on the occupier the greater the duty the occupier owed that entrant.

The Common Law Position

Thus, under the pre-1995 common law position, entrants were divided into the following categories:

(1) *Contractual invitees*—these entrants gained access to the occupier's property under a contract. Under the common law the duty owed to such entrants would very much depend on the terms of the contract under which they entered the property. If the contract was silent on the issue then the duty of the occupier was to take reasonable care in all the circumstances e.g. *O'Gorman v Ritz (Clonmel) Ltd.* [1947] Ir. Jur. Rep. 35 (HC) where the defendant was found to owe the plaintiff cinema-goer a duty of reasonable care.

(2) *Invitees*—the definition of invitee under the common law was somewhat vague. It would appear that an invitee was a person who was invited (either expressly or implicitly) onto the property. The general duty owed to such invitees was to warn such persons of unusual dangers of which he or she knows or ought to know e.g. *Doyle v Magill* [1999] 2 I.L.R.M. 66.

(3) *Licensees*—such entrants were defined as those persons permitted onto another's property, but who did not provide any material benefit to the occupier e.g. *Ellis v Fulham B.C.* [1938] 1 K.B. 359.

(4) *Trespassers*—a trespasser was defined as any person who enters onto another's property in the absence of any invitation or permission from the occupier of the property. Under the common law, an occupier owed a trespasser an even lesser duty than that owed to invitees and licensees. The occupier simply had a duty not to act in such a manner as to intentionally or recklessly injure the trespasser, where the presence of the trespasser on the property was known or ought to have been known by the occupier e.g. *Coffey v McEvoy* [1912] 2 I.R. 290.

The contractual invitee was owed the highest duty of care (reasonableness) while the trespasser was owed the lowest. The standard of care owed towards trespassers was minimal particularly in cases involving child-trespassers. Confusion was introduced to this area by the Supreme Court decision in *McNamara v ESB* [1975] I.R. 1. In that case, an 11 year old boy who climbed over a wire fence surrounding an electrical transformer slipped from the roof of the station. As he fell, his hand came into contact with a live power line and he was severely injured. The boy was a trespasser and the danger involved—the power line—was an obvious one. However, entry into the site was facilitated by the fact that the fence was under repair. Instead of following the categorical approach as outlined above, the court applied general negligence principles when answering the question whether the plaintiff was entitled compensation. The Supreme Court held that it was reasonably foreseeable that children might enter the premises unless reasonable steps were taken to prevent such entry. The fact that the fence was under repair, making access easier, meant that the defendants had not taken all reasonable steps to prevent entry. The defendant was liable for the injuries of the plaintiff.

The decision in *McNamara* effectively altered the standard of care owed to all categories of entrant. As a consequence of the decision, trespassers were afforded much greater protection much to the consternation of landowners/occupiers.

The Occupiers' Liabilty Act 1995

Following the Supreme Court's decision in *McNamara*, the position of landowners and occupiers appeared quite precarious. All landowners and occupiers were fearful that the decision in *McNamara* would create an appalling vista whereby they would be held liable for any injury suffered by an entrant (regardless of his status). From their point of view it was clear that reform of the law in this area was necessary.

Key Definitions

"Danger"

Under s.1(1) of the Act an action can only be brought where the damage is caused due to the state of the premises in question. Thus, any injuries caused by activities on the premises will fall within the traditional rules of negligence and outside the scope of the Act. In *Hackett v Calla Associates Ltd* [2004] I.E.H.C. 336; the plaintiff lost the sight in one eye after being struck by a weapon carried by a bouncer in a nightclub. It was held that the injury was not caused by a danger due to the state of the premises and thus was not a claim that came within the duty of care imposed by s.3 of the Occupiers' Liability Act 1995.

"Occupier"

Section 1(1), in defining an occupier, places great emphasis on the amount of control which the occupier exercises over the premises in question. The greater the control the individual exercises over the state of the premises, the more likely it is that he or she will be considered an occupier. In *Ashmore v Dublin Land Securities and Dublin Corporation*, Circuit Court, January 14, 2003, the Circuit Court pointed out that ownership did not always equate with control over the property. McMahon J. stated that the essential features of the definition of an occupier were: "... the ability by the party to charged to regulate who comes on to the property and ... the power or the duty such a person may have to repair or fix structural defects on the property ..."

"Premises"

According to s.1(1), the liability of the occupier extends only to the state of the premises. Premises in this context is defined as including any land, water, moveable structures thereon and also includes vessels, trains, aircraft, trains and other means of transport.

"Damage"

According to s.1(1) damage includes loss of property and injury to an animal.

Categories of Entrant

The most significant innovation of the 1995 Act was the creation of new categories of entrant who were owed different duties of care under the Act. The categories under the Act replaced those developed under the common law and effectively repealed the decision in *McNamara*. The following categories were created:

1. VISITORS

Definition

A visitor under the Act is some person who is present on the property with the consent or permission of the occupier. Section 1(1) of the Act defines the following entrants as visitors:

(a) an entrant by virtue of a contractual provision;
(b) an entrant present at the invitation or permission of the occupier;
(c) member of the occupiers' family;
(d) an entrant at the express invitation of a member of the occupiers' family;
(e) an entrant for social purposes connected with the occupier; or a
(f) family member

Sheehy v The Devil's Glen Tours Equestrian Centre Ltd [2001]

The plaintiff had entered onto the defendant's premises, an equestrian centre, in order to avail of the defendant's services. She tripped in the doorway of the premises due to a strip of metal which protruded from the ground.

Held: The plaintiff was a visitor for the purposes of the legislation. She had entered onto the premises with the intention of availing of the commercial services on offer and had been injured by a defect in the state of the premises due to the defendant's failure to take reasonable care. *Sheehy v The Devil's Glen Tours Equestrian Centre Ltd,* High Court, December 10, 2001.

The Occupier's Duty towards Visitors

Key Principle: An occupier owes a duty of care (the common duty of care) towards all visitors with respect to dangers on the premises. The standard of care is similar to that used in common law negligence (s.3(1)).

Heaves v Westmeath CC [2001]

The plaintiff slipped on some rustic steps while walking in the grounds of Belvedere House. The house and grounds was open to the public and the plaintiff had paid an entry fee to enter the premises. The plaintiff had slipped on a step which contained a slight indentation that was partially covered by moss. The plaintiff alleged that he was a visitor for the purposes of the 1995 Act (as he had paid a fee upon entry to the car park on the premises) and, as such, was owed a duty of care which had been breached by the defendant. The defendant contended that the plaintiff was not a visitor but a recreational user (see below) and was not owed a common duty of care.
Held: McMahon J. found that the plaintiff was a visitor for the purposes of the legislation. The fee that had been paid upon entry to the car park amounted to an entry fee as it was paid by the plaintiff and each of his children and it was found that this fee would have been payable even if the plaintiff had arrived on foot. The court held however that while the defendant did owe the plaintiff a duty of care, it had not breached that duty. The defendant had taken reasonable precautions in protecting the public from such dangers. In particular, the court noted that the defendant had appointed personnel to address such risks, the head gardener was found to have a satisfactory cleaning system in place which had worked well for several years. Further, should any difficulty outside his range of competence arise, then outside experts were engaged to solve the difficulty. Thus, the defendant was found to have taken all reasonable steps in relation to the particular risk and consequently was not liable. *Heaves v Westmeath CC,* Circuit Court, October 17, 2001.

Healy v Fleming [2001]

The plaintiff was a punter at the defendant's point-to-point race meeting. She slipped while walking up a steep incline on her way to a tent to get shelter from rain. There was a longer and safer route to the tent, but the plaintiff simply followed the crowd.

Held: The entrant was a contractual invitee (now a visitor under the 1995 Act). The occupier was under a duty to take reasonable care for her safety. There had been no similar accident on the site since 1959. In rejecting the plaintiff's claim, McMahon J. stated that meetings of this type should be "encouraged, rather than discouraged." Consequently, the defendant had not breached the duty of care. *Healy v Fleming* [2001]: 19 Ir. L. Times (ns) 241 (Circuit Court, Kanturk, June 2, 2001).

Key Principle: When determining the level of duty owed, the occupier is normally entitled to expect that the visitor will take reasonable care for his or her own safety (s.3(2)).

Roles v Nathan [1963]

Two chimney sweeps were employed to clean a dilapidated boiler which was smoking. The occupier warned the chimney sweeps that the inspection chamber to the boiler should be sealed before it was lit. They ignored this warning and died when they were overcome with the fumes from the boiler.

Held: The occupier was not liable for the deaths. The chimney sweeps ignored the warnings and the occupier was entitled to expect that this warning, together with the chimney sweeps' expertise as regards the danger, would be sufficient to discharge his duty of care towards them as visitors. *Roles v Nathan* [1963] 1 W.L.R. 117.

Key Principle: Where the visitor enters the premises in the company of another (e.g. a child visitor who enters onto premises with a guardian), the occupier is entitled to expect that the latter will exercise reasonable care in relation to the visitor's activities while on the premises (s.3(2)).

Phipps v Rochester Corporation [1955]

The defendant corporation dug a trench for the purpose of laying down a sewer as part of a housing complex. The trench was left unguarded and open despite the fact that the corporation were aware that children often played nearby. The plaintiff, a five year old boy, fell into the trench while walking with his seven year old sister.

Held: The plaintiff was considered to be a licensee under the common law. The corporation was aware of the children's presence on the land and had never protested. The corporation was under a duty to warn the licensee of imperceptible dangers (in this case, the unguarded trench was considered to be an imperceptible danger to young children). The plaintiff's claim ultimately failed, as the court found that, in considering whether the duty to the licensee had been breached, it was entitled to take into account that:

(a) reasonable parents would not have allowed the plaintiff wander unaccompanied by a responsible adult in such circumstances;
(b) any guardian of the child or the occupier of the land in question would act reasonably in relation to the danger; and
(c) each (guardian of the child and the occupier of the land) is entitled to assume that the other will act reasonably.

In the present case, it was held that while the child was on the land as a licensee, the duty owed to him at common law had not been breached by the defendant. *Phipps v Rochester Corporation* [1955] 1 Q.B. 450.

2. RECREATIONAL USERS

Definition

Section 1(1) of the 1995 Act defines a recreational user as being present on the premises with or without the permission of the occupier (or by his implied invitation) for the purposes of engaging in a recreational activity free of charge (other than a reasonable charge for car parking facilities).

Excluded from this definition are members of the occupier's family ordinarily resident on the premises, entrants present at the express invitation of the occupier or any such member of his family and, entrants present with the permission of the occupier or any such member of his family for social reasons connected with the occupier or his family.

Recreational activity has been defined as any recreational activity conducted in the open air. Such activity includes playing sport, conducting scientific research, exploring caves and visiting sites of historic, traditional, artistic, archaeological, or scientific importance.

Byrne v Dun Laoghaire/Rathdown CC [2001]

The plaintiff was an adult coaching an Under-15 soccer team on a public playing field in July. The plaintiff tripped due to an indentation on the surface of the field and was injured.

Held: The plaintiff was not a visitor but a recreational user by virtue of the fact that he had not received permission from the defendant County Council to train on the field during what was the off-season. Further, the defendant was not found to have acted with reckless disregard in exposing the plaintiff to the danger. *Byrne v Dun Laoghaire/Rathdown CC*, Circuit Court, Smyth P., November 13, 2001.

3. TRESPASSERS

Definition

Key Principle: A trespasser is defined as an entrant who is not a recreational user or visitor.

Williams v TP Wallace Construction Ltd [2002]

The defendant was engaged to construct a shopping centre. During construction, the defendant had used guttering which had been supplied to them by a builders' providers company. The guttering had been distributed by a third company. When difficulties arose with the fitting of the guttering, the builders' providers company asked the plaintiff (general manager of the third company) to come to the site to examine the problem. The plaintiff was brought to the site by the assistant manager of the builders' providers company, where they expected to meet the architect. When they arrived at the site, the architect was not present and the builders were on their break. The plaintiff and the assistant manager told the foreman that they would call back later. On their way out of the site it was alleged that the party met another builder who showed them how to access the guttering via a flat roof. As the plaintiff descended from the roof on a ladder, he slipped and fell as the ladder was not tied or otherwise secured.

Held: The question of how the plaintiff gained access to the roof was critical, as it was essential to determining whether he had permission to climb to the roof. It was clear that the plaintiff had permission to enter the premises (his presence had been requested by the defendant), however this permission did not automatically extend to allowing the plaintiff to wander the site unattended. Morris P. rejected the evidence put forward on behalf of the plaintiff that another worker on the site had assisted him in gaining access to the roof as being an unlikely occurrence. Thus, the plaintiff's presence on the roof was outside the bounds of his invitation and as such he could no longer be considered a visitor at the time of the accident. Having exceeded the confines of his invitation, he was by implication considered a trespasser. The court found that the defendants had not injured the plaintiff intentionally nor had they acted with reckless disregard for his safety in failing to secure the ladder, consequently, they were not considered liable for his injuries. *Williams v TP Wallace Construction Ltd* [2002] 2 I.L.R.M. 63.

Duty owed toward Recreational Users and Trespassers

Key Principle: The duty owed to recreational users and trespassers is the same (s.4). The occupier must avoid intentionally injuring such entrants or from acting with reckless disregard for their safety.

"Recklessness" Defined

In determining whether the occupier has acted recklessly, regard must be had for the surrounding circumstances of each individual case including a number of factors specifically outlined in s.4(2):

  (i) whether the occupier knew or should have known of the existence of the danger on the premises;
 (ii) whether the occupier knew or should have known that the entrant or his property was going to be present on the premises;
(iii) whether the occupier knew or should have known that the entrant or his property was going to be in the vicinity of the danger;
 (iv) whether the danger was one which it might reasonably be expected that the occupier would have provided protection for the entrant or his property;
  (v) the burden on the occupier in eliminating or providing protection from the danger for the entrant or his property having regard to the difficulty, expense or impracticality of doing so, while having regard to the character of the premises and the degree of danger involved;
 (vi) the character of the premises used for recreational activity and the public utility in maintaining the tradition of open access to such premises of such a character for such an activity;

(vii) the conduct of the person, and the care which he or she may reasonably be expected to take for his or her own safety, while on the premises, having regard to his or her knowledge thereof;

(viii) the nature of any warning given by the occupier or another person of the danger; and

(ix) whether or not the person was on the premises in the company of another person (i.e. parent and child) and, if so, the extent of supervision and control the latter might reasonably be expected to exercise over the other's activities.

Key Principle: An occupier is under a duty to warn trespassers and recreational users of "exceptionally unusual" dangers.

Weir-Rodgers v ST Trust Ltd [2005]

The respondent had been sitting near the edge of a cliff admiring the sunset. Entry to the cliff's edge had been facilitated by a fence which had fallen into disrepair. The respondent had followed a well-beaten path to the cliff's edge where she sat down with some friends to view the sunset. When she got up to leave she lost her footing as she slipped on some loose earth close to the edge of the cliff. She fell and was badly injured. In the High Court the respondent was deemed to be recreational user and it was held that the duty owed towards her had been breached. She was awarded €113,000 in damages. The damages were reduced by 25 per cent to take into consideration her contributory negligence.

Held: The Supreme Court overturned the decision of the High Court finding that the lower court had misapplied the appropriate standard, pitching the definition of "recklessness" at a level which was too favourable to the entrant. The court stated that where the danger was "exceptionally unusual and dangerous" then an occupier may be liable for failing to warn the trespasser/recreational user of that danger. *Weir-Rodgers v ST Trust Ltd* [2005] 1 I.L.R.M. 471.

Key Principle: The occupier's knowledge of the likelihood of the entrant's vicinity to the danger may be determinative of the issue.

McGowan v Dun Laoghaire-Rathdown CC and Sandycove Bathers' Association [2004]

The plaintiff had been paralysed when he struck a rock when diving from rocks on the coastline in a popular spot for such activity. The rock was invisible from the surface of the water and there was no warning of the danger in place.

Held: High Court found that the defendants had acted with reckless disregard for the plaintiff's safety. The premises were extremely popular with swimmers and the defendants were aware of such activities. The erection of a warning sign regarding the possibility that such rocks existed would have discharged this duty. Given the nature of the damage and the defendants' knowledge that the entrants would be in the vicinity of the danger, the occupier was under a duty to warn of the danger notwithstanding the fact that the entrant in question was not a visitor. *McGowan v Dun Laoghaire-Rathdown CC and Sandycove Bathers' Association* [2004] High Court, May 7, 2004.

Key Principle: Under s.4 an occupier is entitled to expect that the entrant will take into consideration his or her own safety.

Tomlinson v Congleton B.C. [2004]

The plaintiff was a teenager who entered on to land owned by the local authority. The plaintiff was paralysed after diving into a lake on the land when his head struck the bottom. The local authority had been aware that people entered the property to swim in the lake and had put up signs warning people not to swim there. These signs were often ignored. The local authority planned to plant vegetation around the lake to prevent people gaining access to it however this had not been done at the time of the plaintiff's accident.

Held: The House of Lords found that the occupier could not be under a duty to prevent people taking risks inherent in the activities that they undertook on the land, pointing out that if entrants wish to undertake inherently dangerous activities, that is their affair. In such circumstances there is no obligation on the occupier of such property to warn the entrant of perfectly obvious dangers associated with such activity. *Tomlinson v Congleton B.C.* [2004] 1 A.C. 46.

Warnings

Key Principle: Under s.5, an occupier may, by express agreement or notice, extend his or her duty towards visitors and recreational users.

Furthermore, the occupier may, by express agreement or notice, restrict, modify or exclude his duty to take reasonable care towards visitors. Any such restriction must be reasonable in all the circumstances and where the occupier purports to modify the statutory duty by notice, the occupier must take reasonable steps to bring the notice to the attention of the visitor. The occupier cannot reduce the standard owed to visitors below the statutory standard set for trespassers and recreational users. The warning must be such that it is enough to enable the visitor, by having regard to the warning, to avoid the injury or damage so caused.

White v Blackmore **[1972]**

The deceased was a member of a car racing club. He attended a race where he signed on as a competitor. At the entrance of the site of the race was a sign which stated "Warning to the Public: Motor Racing is dangerous" and excluded liability to "spectators or ticket holders". The deceased entered free as a spectator. He was later killed while watching a race when one of the cars collided with the spectator barrier.
Held: The notice was sufficient to absolve the occupiers of liability. It was directed to the deceased as a spectator and was sufficiently explicit. *White v Blackmore* [1972] 2 Q.B. 651.

10. LIABILITY FOR DEFECTIVE PRODUCTS

INTRODUCTION

There exists both common law and statutory liability for defective products under Irish law. In addition to the principles of negligence, as formulated by Lord Atkin in *Donoghue v Stevenson* [1932] A.C. 562; legislation has been passed by the Oireachtas in the form of the Liability for Defective Products Act 1991 which supplements the common law position.

Both heads of liability differ in their approach to this area. Under negligence, attention is focused on the behaviour of the producer—did he or she act with reasonable care? The legislation on the other hand is not concerned with fault. The 1991 Act concentrates on the condition of the product in question, not the behaviour of the producer. Liability under the Act is strict.

Traditionally, before a plaintiff could succeed in a claim for injury caused as the result of a defective product, he or she would have to establish the existence of a valid contract between the parties. The injured party could only bring an action where privity of contract existed between the producer/manufacturer of the product and the plaintiff. The requirement of privity created difficulties for the plaintiff consumer as he or she may not have had a contract with the original producer of the product i.e. before the product would have reached the consumer it may have been the subject of a number of transactions, leaving the ultimate consumer far removed (in contractual terms) from the original producer. Some exceptions to this principle did exist e.g. presence of fraud on the part of the producer, failure to warn regarding defects which were known at the time and so forth.

COMMON LAW LIABILITY

Key Principle: In the absence of a reasonable possibility of intermediate inspection, the manufacturer of a defective product will be liable to the ultimate consumer for all reasonably foreseeable injury caused by that product.

Donoghue v Stevenson [1932]

The plaintiff drank ginger beer from a dark coloured bottle which was bought for her by a friend in a café. The plaintiff became ill upon discovering the remains of a decomposed snail in the bottle and brought an action seeking damages from the defendant manufacturer. **Held:** Despite the absence of a contract between the parties, the court found that there existed a relationship of legal proximity between the plaintiff and the defendant that gave rise to the existence of a duty of care. The defendant should have foreseen that his negligence in the manufacture of the ginger beer would cause injury to the plaintiff (the ultimate consumer) particularly in a situation where it was not reasonable (due to the sealing of the ginger beer in a dark coloured bottle) to expect that an intermediate inspection of the product would take place before reaching the plaintiff. *Donoghue v Stevenson* [1932] A.C. 562.

Key Principle: The common law definition of manufacturer includes repairers, assemblers and even retailers of products.

Stennett v Hancock and Peters [1939]

The plaintiff was a pedestrian struck by a flange which had become detached from the wheel of the first-named defendant's lorry. It was established in evidence that the flange had earlier been negligently repaired by the second-named defendants. **Held:** The repairers were found liable as manufacturers under the principle established in *Donoghue*. It was foreseeable that should they failed to carry out their duties responsibly, other road users could be injured. *Stennett v Hancock and Peters* [1939] 2 All E.R. 578.

Key Principle: Liability in negligence is not limited to the ultimate consumer, but may include any member of the public who should have been in the reasonable contemplation of the manufacturer at the time the product was produced.

Barnett v H. & J. Packer & Co Ltd [1940]

The plaintiff confectioner was injured while placing a tray of sweets on display in his shop window. It transpired that one of the negligently produced sweets had contained a piece of wire which cut the plaintiff's fingers causing the plaintiff to contract blood poisoning.

Held: The court found that the producer's duty was not limited to the ultimate consumer of the product (in this case customers of the plaintiff) but to all those whom he or she could reasonably foresee could be injured by the his or her negligent actions or omissions.The plaintiff clearly came within this category and was entitled to damages from the defendant. *Barnett v H. & J. Packer & Co Ltd* [1940] 3 All E.R. 575.

Brown v Cotterill [1934]

The plaintiff was a young child who was injured when a tombstone collapsed and injured her.

Held: The stone mason who erected the tombstone was found liable in negligence for the child's injuries. The court stated that the mason had a duty to all those who lawfully might enter the graveyard and be injured by the falling tombstone. *Brown v Cotterill* (1934) 51 T.L.R. 21 (KBD).

The Duty to Warn

Key Principle: At common law the manufacturer of a product has a duty to warn the unsuspecting public of any foreseeable dangers associated with the use of the product. Furthermore, the manufacturer will be liable for the foreseeable misuse of the product and must act accordingly to discharge his or her duty of care.

O'Byrne v Gloucester [1998]

The plaintiff, a girl aged fifteen, was badly burned when her skirt came into contact with a gas heater in her home. The plaintiff brought an action against the manufacturers of the skirt alleging that they had been negligent in failing to provide her with an adequate warning regarding the dangers connected with the product, i.e. its high flammability.

Held: The Supreme Court upheld the plaintiff's claim. The danger in question was one which should have been foreseeable to the defendants and they were found to have owed the plaintiff a duty of care. This duty could have been discharged easily by simply attaching a warning label to the garment. *O'Byrne v Gloucester*, Supreme Court, November 3, 1988.

Cassells v Marks & Spencer [1999]

The plaintiff was a five year old girl who was injured when her cotton dress caught fire as a result of her proximity to an open fire. On purchase, the dress had contained a warning label which stated, "Keep away from fire." However, the dress fell below minimum flammability standards required for children's nightwear.

Held: The defendants had acted appropriately and were not negligent. A clear warning had been attached to the clothing. The court stated that the garment in question need not meet the flammability standards set for nightwear as the dress was mainly for outdoor use, thereby reducing the chances of it coming into contact with fire. The defendants had discharged their duty of care under the circumstances. *Cassells v Marks & Spencer*, High Court, March 25, 1999 (Barr J.).

Key Principle: The plaintiff must not only prove that the defendant was negligent in failing to warn regarding the danger but also that it was that failure to warn which caused the injury.

Duffy v Rooney and Dunnes Stores (Dundalk) Ltd [1998]

The plaintiff was a two year old child who was severely burned when the coat she was wearing came in contact with an open fire. The coat contained no warning that it was highly flammable and that it should be kept away from fire.

Held: Notwithstanding the fact that at the time of the accident there were no statutory regulation regarding the need for such warnings, the court found that the manufacturer had been negligent in failing to attach the warning. Laffoy J. was of the opinion that a reasonably prudent manufacturer/retailer should have attached a warning for the following reasons: open fires were common in houses in Ireland at that time, young children are commonly dressed by their parents inside the house; young children were unpredictable and were not aware of dangers posed by open fires; accidents involving fire are most serious and the labelling of garments involves very low costs. However, even though the court found that the failure to warn was negligent behaviour on the part of the manufacturer, the plaintiff's claim failed on the issue of causation. The plaintiff had not established that the retailer's negligence caused the injury, as evidence was introduced which showed that even had there been a label, the plaintiff would still have been wearing the coat inside. The court drew this inference from the fact that at the time of the accident, the plaintiff was wearing trousers and a sweatshirt to which warning labels were attached. *Duffy v Rooney and Dunnes Stores (Dundalk) Ltd*, unreported, Supreme Court, April 23, 1998.

STATUTORY LIABILITY

Introduction

The Liability for Defective Products Act 1991 was introduced as a direct result of a European Union Directive in 1985. The main feature of the legislation is that it introduces a regime of no fault or strict liability. As Burton J. in *A v National Blood Authority* [2001] 3 All E.R. 289 put it, liability under the legislation is "defect-based and not fault-based."

Rationale

The legislation was enacted by way of supplemental protection for consumers. While at the common law consumers could seek a remedy under contract or tort law principles these methods of redress were not without their drawbacks. As outlined earlier, contract law was only of limited usefulness i.e. those consumers who had a contract with the producer. The difficulties in proving a duty of care, fault and causation would discourage consumers from bringing claims particularly where the sums being claimed were small in amount. The preamble to the 1991 legislation provided that the legislation was the fairest means of distributing the loss suffered by a consumer as a result of his use of a defective product. The legislation—by introducing a regime of strict liability—is intended to protect the weaker party lured by the packaging and advertising of the producer in circumstances where the consumer has no opportunity of inspecting the goods prior to purchase.

Another rationale for the adoption of strict liability is what is known as the "enterprise" basis of liability. This theory provides that the proper cost to a manufacturer includes the cost of the damage caused by a defect in that product (See: *Escola v Coca-Cola Bottling Co of Fresno* [1944] 150 P.2d 436. Yet another rationale for the introduction of strict liability legislation is the theory that such a move will act as a deterrent to the producers of defective products. Such a move will reduce the flow of such goods into the marketplace which is in the interest of society as a whole.

DEFINITIONS

"Producer"

Section 2(3) also provides that a "producer" under the Act will be any person who is:

(a) the manufacturer/producer of a finished product;
(b) the manufacturer/producer of any raw material or component part of the product;
(c) the person who carries out the initial processing of a product of the soil, fisheries and game;
(d) any person who puts his name or trademark to a product;
(e) any person who imports the product into a member state from outside the EU in the ordinary course of business.

Section 2(3) states that where the actual producer cannot be reasonably identified by the consumer, the supplier of the product will be found liable if:

(a) the injured party requests the supplier to identify the producer;
(b) that request is made within a reasonable time after the damage occurs;
(c) the supplier fails, within a reasonable time after receiving the request, either to comply with the request or to identify the person who supplied the product to him.

The definition of producer is very wide. It includes not only the manufacturer of the product, but also any defendant who lends a brand or trademark to a product or who is the first importer of the product into the EU. Furthermore, s.2(3) will ensure, at the very least, that the purchaser/importer of a product will keep appropriate records as to who supplied the product to them—otherwise the supplier could be fixed with liability where the manufacturer cannot be identified.

"Damage"

Damage is defined under s.1(1) as meaning:

(a) death or personal injury, or;

(b) loss of, damage to, or destruction of property (other than the product itself) provided such property was used for private consumption.

The legislation provides in point (b) above, that compensation will not be available for loss of the product itself as this is deemed to be pure economic loss. Compensation is not available where the damage caused is below €445. Where damages exceed this threshold, only the excess is recoverable.

"Defective Product"

Under s.5 of the Act a product is defective if it fails to provide the safety which a person is entitled to expect. Safety is not what is actually expected by the public at large, but what they are entitled to expect. The question is one of "legitimate expectation" rather than "entitled expectation".

Section 5(1) provides that a product is defective if it fails to provide the safety which a person is entitled to expect, taking all circumstances into account, including:

(a) *the presentation of the product*—if a producer represents that his or her product will provide the user with a great deal of safety benefits, then the producer will be liable where the product fails to live up to this expectation

(b) *the use to which it could be reasonably expected it would be put*—a producer is only liable where the product is put to its reasonable use

(c) *the time the product was put into circulation*—the time at which the product is purchased could be very important. A consumer must expect some wear and tear.

Commentary

The focus on the safety of the product from the point of view of what the consumer is entitled to expect is an important yet subtle distinction from the common law. The test is not simply one of reasonableness as in negligence simpliciter (although often the two standards will go hand in hand). By focusing on the expectations of the consumer, the producer may be liable where he or she has falsely raised the hopes of the consumer and the product then fails to meet with those standards.

Key Principle: A product is defective where it fails to attain the level of safety that the consumer is entitled to expect taking all the circumstances into account.

A v National Blood Authority [2001]

The plaintiff brought an action under product liability legislation in England (The Consumer Protection Act 1987). The plaintiff was infected with Hepatitis C from blood transfusions organised by the defendant. The defendant argued that risk of the blood being contaminated was an unavoidable one as they had taken all reasonable precautions in testing the blood and no test existed at the time that would have detected the contamination. In other words, the state of medical knowledge at that time meant that the contamination was undetectable. The plaintiff argued that as liability under the legislation was strict, the reasonableness of the defendant's behaviour was irrelevant—the statute focused on the condition of the product rather than on the behaviour of the producer. Thus the key question was—what exactly was meant by the words *taking all circumstances into account* (similar to s.5) when determining the safety the consumer was entitled to expect. The defendant argued that the question whether the harm could have been avoided was central to determining whether the product was defective and therefore was a "relevant circumstance" to be taken into account. It was the defendant's contention that the public could not legitimately expect that the defendant should be made liable for defects which were unavoidable, particularly when one considered the utility of the product involved.

Held: The plaintiff's action was successful. The public were not aware—unlike now—of the risks associated with such blood products. Therefore, they were not expecting the unattainable when they expected that the blood products would be safe. If they were not aware of the dangers, how could they know about the impossibility of discovering the contamination? Burton J. then expressed the view that in order to give true effect to the strict liability nature of the legislation "all circumstances" in the context of assessing defectiveness should be interpreted as "all relevant circumstances". *A v National Blood Authority* [2001] 3 All E.R. 289.

Bogle v McDonald's Restaurants [2002]

A number of cases arose where plaintiffs were injured after purchasing coffee from the defendant. The plaintiffs had been burned when the coffee spilled and it was alleged that the product i.e. the container in which the coffee was contained was defective—the lid could be better fitted and the serving of the coffee at such a high temperature rendered it defective.

Held: The defendant was not liable in the circumstances. The protection the plaintiffs were entitled to expect was that a warning be placed on the cups that the lid was sealed insofar as was possible and that staff were trained in relation to same. The consumer was not entitled to expect that the coffee would be 100 per cent safe and the consumer accepted that in order to produce the coffee it had to be done at a hot temperature and therefore accepted the risks associated therewith. *Bogle v McDonald's Restaurants* [2002] E.W.H.C. 490 (Q.B.)

Abouzaid v Mothercare (UK) [2000]

A 12 year old boy was injured in the eye while helping his mother fasten a sleeping bag to his brother's push chair. The fastenings were elastic, and one of the hooks snapped back and caught him in the eye.

Held: The sleeping bag and the fastening mechanism were not considered as safe as the consumer was entitled to expect. Liability could have been avoided if the defendant had supplied instructions explaining how users of the product could avoid such injuries. *Abouzaid v Mothercare (UK)* [2000] All E.R. (D) 2436 (CA).

"Defences"

Section 6 of the Act provides a number of defences to a claim by a consumer under the legislation:

(1) *not responsible for circulation*—a producer will not be liable where he or she can show that he or she did not put the product into circulation.

(2) *defect not in existence at the time*—a producer will not be made liable if he or she can prove that the defect did not exist when he or she put the product into circulation or that the defect did not arise until after he or she put the product into circulation.

(3) *not manufactured for a commercial purpose*—a producer will not be made liable where he or she produces the product for a non-commercial purpose.

(4) *mandatory requirements*—a producer will not be made liable where the defect arises because of some change he or she had to make to it in order that it complied with a requirement of law. Thus, if a product's ingredients must under national law, comply with certain requirements, and that change renders the product defective, then the producer may have a defence.

(5) *lack of scientific/technical knowledge or the developmental risks defence*—the producer can relieve himself or herself of liability if he or she can establish that the defect was not identifiable at the time he or she put the product into circulation because of the lack of scientific/technical knowledge at the time.

(6) *defect attributable to product in which the product is fitted*—if the producer can establish that the defect was the result of the design of the product into which his or her component product was fitted, he or she may avoid liability.

Commentary

The single most dramatic change introduced by the Liability for Defective Products Act 1991 was the introduction of the principle of strict liability into an area of tort law that had traditionally been governed by fault principles. As a consequence, the consumer can now succeed in an action against a producer where he or she can establish that the product was defective and that he or she suffered as a consequence of that defect. The fault of the producer is no longer a necessary element in establishing liability.

The Act supplements and does not replace the existing rights available to the consumer (s.11) and does to a large degree, have the effect of levelling the playing field in terms of litigation between commercial enterprises creating products for financial profit, and members of the public injured as a result of defects contained within such products. In some respects, it is submitted that the 1991 Act succeeds in this aim. The introduction of strict liability will no doubt make it easier for a plaintiff to succeed in a claim, notwithstanding that the plaintiff's difficulty in establishing the causative link between the defect in the product and the damage still remains. The broad definition of producer shall ensure that producers will not be able to avoid liability by pointing the finger at manufacturers that reside outside the jurisdiction of the European Union. Further, the legislation will deter enterprises from easily lending their brand name or trademark to inferior products in pursuit of a greater profit.

However, the dearth of reported case law on the Act (and in the UK under its equivalent the Consumer Protection Act 1987) would seem to indicate that its introduction has not revolutionised the law. It may be that such has been the deterrent effect of the Act, that very few cases have been litigated under the legislation. However, it is clear that the effectiveness of the strict liability element of the Act has been somewhat watered down with the introduction of a wide range of defences being made available to the producer under s.7. For example, a producer will not attract liability where he or she can establish that the state of scientific and technical knowledge at the time could not discover the defect. Thus, it would appear to introduce the general standard of reasonableness into the equation, which is far removed from the principles of strict liability.

The importance of the traditional common law action of negligence cannot be dismissed. In a great many cases, establishing the existence of a duty of care which has been breached will not prove insurmountable, leaving the issue of causation which is common to both the strict and fault liability regimes. Indeed, in certain circumstances an action in negligence may be the only avenue of redress available to the consumer. For example, under the legislation a producer could relieve himself or herself of liability by insisting that the defect in the product was caused by changes made to it in order that it may comply with certain regulatory standards (otherwise known as the mandatory requirements defence). However, it is unclear whether such a defence would always apply at common law. If the defect arising from the changes made should have been foreseeable by the producer, then he or she will be liable in negligence for allowing the product to be placed on the market following such changes.

11. EMPLOYERS' LIABILITY FOR OCCUPATIONAL INJURIES

INTRODUCTION

Given the amount of time individuals spend in the workplace it is not surprising that a great many injuries are suffered by individuals while working. Consequently, an employer is vulnerable to claims for personal injury from his or her employees. An employer's liability can arise under a number of different headings. First, under the common law, an employer is directly liable in negligence to his or her employees. Secondly, an employer may be liable under the common law to third parties for the negligent actions of his or her employees under the doctrine of vicarious liability. Thirdly, an employer may be liable under statute in the form of the Safety, Health and Welfare at Work Acts 1989–2005.

Traditionally, employers were a protected species under the common law in this regard. The cultivation of industry was considered essential to the development of society and the economy and as such the courts were loathe to place liability for injuries caused to employees in the workplace on the shoulders of employers. Thus, in response to any action in negligence by an employee the employer could rely on what was known as the unholy trinity of defences namely, the doctrine of common employment, contributory negligence and *volenti non fit injuria*. The doctrine of common employment implied into all contracts of employment that the employee accepted the risks incidental to that employment, including the possibility of being injured by a fellow employee (*Priestly v Fowler* (1837) 3 M & W 1). The defence of contributory negligence provided that should it be proven that the employee contributed in any way to his or her injuries, then he or she could not recover any compensation for the resulting injuries. While the defence of *volenti non fit injuria* provided that where the employee was aware of the risk and continued to work, then he or she was said to have consented to running the risk of the injury.

However, towards the end of the nineteenth century judicial attitudes began to change and the courts became more protective of the injured employee. In *General Cleaning Contractors v Christmas* [1953] A.C. 180, Lord Oaksey explained this shift in attitude when he said:

> "Workmen are not in a position of employers. Their duties are
> not performed in the calm atmosphere of a board room with
> the advice of experts. They have to make their decisions on
> narrow window sills and other places of danger and in circum-
> stances in which the dangers are obscured by repetition."

The doctrine of common employment was abolished by s.1 of the Law
Reform (Personal Injuries) Act 1958 (No. 38). The defence of contributory negligence has been amended under s.34(1) of the Civil
Liability Act 1961 and no longer does it provide a complete defence to
an action in negligence. Finally, the defence of *volenti* has been sub-
stantially changed under s.34(1)(b) of the Civil Liability Act 1961. The
standard of care now expected of an employer is one to take reasonable
care for the welfare of his or her employees during their employment.

1. THE DUTY OF CARE

Introduction

The duty of care is not usually a controversial issue where an employee
is seeking recovery in damages for an injury which has resulted from
his or her employer's negligence. Where an employer and employee
relationship exists and an employee suffers an occupational injury,
questions of foreseeability, proximity of relationship and policy do not
normally prove to be insurmountable hurdles to a plaintiff given the
legal relationship which exists between the parties.

Key Principle: An employer does not owe a duty of care to an
employee where that employee has developed a psychiatric illness due
to an irrational worry that he or she may contract a disease in the future
as a result of being negligently exposed to the risk of contracting that
disease by his or her employer.

Fletcher v Commissioner of Public Works **[2003]**

The plaintiff was employed as a general operative in Leinster House.
One of his main duties was to assist plumbers and various tradesmen
in the maintenance of the heating system in the building. The piping
system was covered with lagging containing asbestos fibres. The
defendant did not warn the plaintiff of the risks that he was being
exposed to nor did it provide him with any protective clothing.

Consequently, the plaintiff inhaled quantities of asbestos fibres. Having been informed of the risk he had been exposed to, the plaintiff was referred to a consultant respiratory physician and was told that he had not been physically injured in any way and that the chance of developing an illness as a result of his exposure was "very remote". The plaintiff was not comforted and continued to worry that he would develop a respiratory illness. This irrational worry led to the development of a psychiatric illness known as "reactive anxiety neurosis" for which the plaintiff sought compensation.

Held: This case was a novel one and was not a case of "nervous shock" as the psychiatric injury was not one that was shock-induced. In determining whether a duty of care was owed to the plaintiff, the court held that the damage was foreseeable (notwithstanding the "irrationality" of the plaintiff) and there was a proximate relationship between the parties by virtue of the employment relationship. Thus the court emphasized that policy would play a crucial role in determining whether recovery for damage of this nature should be recognized. The court concluded that given the remote chance that the plaintiff would contract a respiratory illness the employer could not be said to have owed a duty of care for the psychiatric injury which the plaintiff contracted because he irrationally feared that he would contract that illness. *Fletcher v Commissioner of Public Works* [2003] I.L.R.M. 94.

2. THE STANDARD OF CARE

Key Principle: The duty an employer owes towards his or her employees is to take reasonable care for their safety in all the circumstances of their employment.

Brady v Beckmann Instruments (Galway) Inc **[1986]**

The plaintiff employee contracted a rare form of dermatitis as a result of inhaling fumes in the workplace. It was proven that the safety precautions taken by the defendant were exemplary. Further, no evidence existed whereby similar individuals had contracted dermatitis having been exposed to the levels that the plaintiff had been.

Held: The defendant was not liable. The evidence indicated that contracting the dermatitis as the plaintiff had done, was unique and improbable and could not have been reasonably foreseen by the defendant. *Brady v Beckmann Instruments (Galway) Inc* [1986] I.L.R.M. 361 (SC).

Key Principle: The duty owed by an employer to his or her employees is personal and is non-delegable. Thus, it is no defence for the employer to state that he or she had conferred the responsibility of executing that duty carefully to another competent party.

Wilsons and Clyde Coal Co Ltd v English [1938]

The plaintiff was a miner who was injured in the defendant's mine. He was crushed as he was leaving the mine at the end of his shift by a haulage plant which should not have been in operation at a time when miners would be travelling through the mine. The defendant argued that they were not liable as they had appointed a qualified manager over the mine whose responsibility it was to ensure the safety of the workers.

Held: The court rejected the defendant's claim, stating that the duty to provide a safe system of work was non-delegable and the defendant could not escape responsibility by passing the obligation on to another employee. *Wilsons and Clyde Coal Co Ltd v English* [1938] A.C. 57.

Connolly v Dundalk UDC and Mahon & McPhilips [1990]

The plaintiff was injured when he inhaled gas while working as a caretaker at the first-named defendant's waterworks. He had inhaled the gas as a result of a leak in one of the pipes which had been badly fitted. The second-named defendant had been engaged by the first-named defendant to install and maintain the piping system. The plaintiff alleged that his employer had failed to provide him with a safe place of work. The first-named defendant argued that it could not be held liable for the plaintiff's injuries as the maintenance of the piping system was the responsibility of the independent contractor.

Held: The first-named defendant could not avoid liability for breach of duty by engaging an independent contractor (no matter how expert) to carry out this duty on its behalf. *Connolly v Dundalk UDC and Mahon & McPhilips* [1990] 2 I.R. 1.

Key Principle: An employer who has purchased equipment from a reputable manufacturer or supplier which causes injury to an employee due to some latent defect contained therein will not be liable for injuries caused by the defective equipment. This is an exception to the principle of non-delegability.

Davie v New Merton Board Mills Ltd [1959]

The plaintiff was a fitter who, while hammering a chisel, was injured when a particle of the chisel broke off entering his eye. A reputable firm had sold it to a well established firm of suppliers who, in turn, had provided it to the defendant employers. The injured plaintiff brought an action in negligence against his employer.

Held: The employer was not liable to the employee. There was no evidence that the employer's system of internal checking was in any way deficient. Notwithstanding the non-delegable nature of the employer's duties the court stated that the principle of non-delegability should not be extended to such situations. *Davie v New Merton Board Mills Ltd* [1959] A.C. 604.

HEADS OF LIABILITY

Whether an employee has a cause of action in negligence against his or her employer for injuries sustained at work will depend on the circumstances of the particular case. However, the common law duties imposed on the employer may be identified as follows:

(a) Provision of a safe place of work;
(b) Provision of competent staff;
(c) Provision of safe equipment;
(d) Provision of a safe system of work.

(a) Duty to Provide a Safe Place of Work

Key Principle: The employer is under a duty to take all reasonable care to provide and maintain a safe place of work for his or her employees. This includes a duty to provide a safe means of entry and egress to the workplace.

Latimer v AEC Ltd [1953]

A factory floor was flooded. The floor became very slippery as the water mixed with an oily liquid. Some of the defendant's employees were instructed to cover the floor with sawdust but left a portion uncovered. Unfortunately, the plaintiff slipped on a portion of the spillage that remained. The plaintiff argued that the reasonable prudent factory owner would have shut the factory down completely until the spillage was cleaned up.

Held: The defendant was not liable in negligence. The defendant acted reasonably in the circumstances and took all reasonable precautions to deal with the danger. *Latimer v AEC Ltd* [1953] 2 All E.R. 449.

Key Principle: The scope of the employer's duty to provide a safe place of work may also extend to the premises of third parties.

Mulcare v Southern Health Board [1988]

The plaintiff was employed as "home help" by the defendant. She hurt her leg while visiting the home of an elderly woman. Her injuries were caused as a result of the floor surface in the woman's house which was in poor condition. The plaintiff alleged that the defendant had failed in its duty to provide her with a safe place of work.
Held: The defendant was not found liable for the plaintiff's injuries. The plaintiff had been visiting the house for seven years and had never been injured. The court was of the view that the house was not in so poor a condition that would place an obligation on the defendant to require the old woman to choose either to renovate her home or lose the home help service. *Mulcare v Southern Health Board* [1988] I.L.R.M. 689 (HC).

Barclay v An Post [1998]

The plaintiff was a postman who injured his back as a result of delivering post to an area of houses and apartments which were fitted with low letterboxes not more than a few inches off the ground. Following his return to work after his injury the plaintiff was employed on overtime to deliver post to some 350 houses, all of which had low level letterboxes. The plaintiff suffered a recurrence of his back problems and aggravated the earlier injury.
Held: The defendant employer had acted reasonably in dealing with the low letterboxes. It had succeeded in having changes made to the building regulations and the planning code regarding the proper height and specifications for such letterboxes. However, the defendant did fail in its duty of care to ensure that, in the short term after the plaintiff's original injury, he did not take up duties which would put undue and extraordinary strain on his back. The employer was held liable for the aggravated injury suffered by the plaintiff in these circumstances. *Barclay v An Post* [1998] 2 I.L.R.M. 285.

(b) Duty to Provide Competent Staff

Key Principle: The employer is under a duty to his or her employees to take all reasonable care in the selection of his or her workers. This duty includes the obligation to monitor all employees during the course of their employment to ensure that they do not represent an unreasonable danger to their fellow employees.

Hough v Irish Base Metals Ltd [1967]

The plaintiff was burned when some of his work colleagues placed a gas fire next to him as part of a prank. This was not the first time that a prank of this nature had been played by employees in the workplace. **Held:** The employer had not breached the duty to provide competent staff. There was no evidence that the employer could have reasonably detected that this prank had been played before. The system of supervision employed by the defendant was found to be adequate. The defendant was not on notice of such behavior as it had never been reported nor was there any evidence that the employer should have been on notice of such behavior. *Hough v Irish Base Metals Ltd,* Supreme Court, December 8, 1967.

(c) Duty to Provide Proper Equipment

Key Principle: The employer is under an obligation to provide proper and safe equipment to his or her employees. The employer must also ensure that any such equipment is maintained to a reasonable standard.

Heeney v Dublin Corporation [1991]

In 1985, a fireman died when he inhaled fumes while fighting a fire in a building. The deceased had not been provided with a breathing apparatus which would have prevented his death. Such a breathing apparatus had been first introduced to certain crews in 1977, yet the deceased's unit had not been provided with such equipment at the time of his death.

Held: The fire authority was found liable in an action for fatal injuries. The delay in providing this vital equipment to the deceased and his unit was unacceptable. The court further rejected the authority's argument that the deceased should have waited outside the burning building until a fully equipped fire unit arrived on the scene. In the absence of any instruction from his superiors, the deceased had to act as he saw fit as a professional fireman. *Heeney v Dublin Corporation,* High Court, May 16, 1991.

Rogers v Bus Átha Cliath [2000]

The plaintiff was a city bus driver for the defendant company. He was assaulted while driving his bus. He brought an action in negligence against his employers for inter alia failing to provide him with the proper equipment necessary for his job. Specifically, the plaintiff argued that the failure to provide the drivers of city buses with suitable protective units while driving was a negligent failure on his employer's part. The issue of attacks on drivers had been identified by the defendants for a number of years. They had developed many designs for such a protective unit, but a suitable design which could comfortably sit and protect the driver could not be decided upon by the drivers' union and the defendant. Eventually, after a number of years, a suitable alternative was agreed upon and the defendant had begun to implement its installation into all buses. Unfortunately, the plaintiff's bus had not been fitted with the agreed protective unit at the time of his assault.

Held: The defendant had acted reasonably at every step of the process. It had identified the problem of the security of its drivers a number of years previously. It commissioned the design of a number of protective units and had consulted the drivers' union regarding each design. Having eventually reached an agreement with the union, the defendant set about implementing the installation process. *Rogers v Bus Átha Cliath,* Circuit Court, January 17, 2000.

(d) Duty to Provide a Safe System of Work

If the method prescribed by the employer to carry out the work is unsafe then he or she may be liable in negligence as a result of any injuries that may result e.g. proper instructions on how to use equipment and protective clothing, organisation of the workplace, warnings regarding hazards and so forth. As Devlin L.J. noted in *Dixon v Cementation Co Ltd* [1960] 3 All E.R. 417 at 419:

> "There may be cases in which the plaintiff will not get very far with an allegation of unsafe system of work unless he can show some practicable alternative, but there are also cases ...

in which a plaintiff can fairly say: 'If this is dangerous, then there must be some other way, that can be found by a prudent employer, of doing it, and it is not for me to advise that way or to say what it is."

Key Principle: The employer must do all that is reasonably necessary to ensure that the method or system by which the employee is expected to carry out his or her work is safe.

Withers v Perry Chain Co [1961]

The plaintiff contracted dermatitis as a result of coming into contact with grease on a regular basis during the course of her work. Upon discovering her ailment, the defendant offered her work which was the driest available. Unfortunately, she contracted dermatitis once again and brought an action against the defendant for failing to implement a safe system of work by exposing her to the risk of contracting the disease for a second time.

Held: The employer had acted reasonably at all times. Upon learning of her affliction she had been moved without protest to an area where the work was much more suitable. The court found that there was nothing else the employer could do given the nature of the work (other than dismissing her) in order to avoid the risk of her contracting the disease. *Withers v Perry Chain Co* [1961] 1 W.L.R. 1314.

General Cleaning Contractors v Christmas [1953]

The plaintiff was employed by the defendant as a window cleaner. He was advised by the defendant that he should use the "sill method" of cleaning windows upstairs. This involved the plaintiff standing on the sill and holding onto the sash of the open window while cleaning it. While employing this method, a window caught his fingers and he fell injuring himself.

Held: The defendant was liable for the plaintiff's injuries as the system of work employed by the defendant was clearly unsafe. While it was established that the defendant could not have provided the plaintiff with ropes in the circumstances, the defendant could have and should have at the very least, checked the safety of all the windows and possibly have provided the plaintiff with wedges to insert in the windows to ensure that they did not shut. The failure by the employer to take these precautions amounted to negligence. *General Cleaning Contractors v Christmas* [1953] A.C. 180.

(i) *Manual Handling*

Key Principle: An employer may be found liable in negligence where he or she requires an employee to carry excessive weights as part of his or her work and as a result, the employee suffers an injury.

Kirby v South Eastern Health Board [1993]

A nurse injured her back and neck while turning a patient over in his bed. The plaintiff argued that this procedure (approved by the defendant) was negligent as it exposed her to injury. Evidence was introduced which established that this procedure was recognised in the 1970s and 1980s as being capable of causing injury and should no longer be followed.
Held: The defendant was liable as it had, or ought to have, known of the dangers inherent in the procedure and yet had not taken reasonable steps to alter it. *Kirby v South Eastern Health Board*, unreported, High Court, Trinity & Michaelmas Terms, 1993 at 234.

Key Principle: The employer will be liable if he or she has not given the employee reasonable instruction on how to carry the load.

Lynch v Dublin Corporation [1991]

The plaintiff was injured while lifting a wheelbarrow containing tools onto a trailer. A fellow employee let the wheelbarrow drop thereby injuring the plaintiff. The plaintiff argued that the process was an unsafe system of work and that the employer was liable.
Held: The court rejected the plaintiff's assertion on the basis that any other conclusion would lead to a situation where "all manual work would have to stop". The court did however, find the employer vicariously liable (for the acts of the other employee) and for not providing the employees with proper training in lifting techniques. *Lynch v Dublin Corporation*; unreported, High Court, Hilary and Easter Terms 1991 at 228.

Key Principle: Training related to workplace safety must be regularly updated.

Firth v South Eastern Health Board [1994]

The plaintiff was a nurse with the defendants since 1970 until 1990. In 1970, she received training as to how a patient should be properly lifted. In 1990, she injured her back whilst carrying out this procedure. It transpired that the method of training she received in 1970 regarding lifting had become outdated and in material published in 1985 it was advised that the procedure was "to be avoided where possible." Evidence was introduced which stated that the plaintiff should have been retrained since 1970.

Held: The defendants had been negligent in failing to keep up to date with training techniques and had therefore exposed the plaintiff to unreasonable risk of back injury. *Firth v South Eastern Health Board* (High Court, July 27, 1994).

(ii) *Stress-related Illness*

Key Principle: An employer may owe a duty of care to an employee suffering from a stress-related illness where it can be proven that the occurrence of the illness was foreseeable.

Walker v Northumberland CC [1995]

The plaintiff had been working as a social worker for 15 years. By its very nature, the job was stressful. He requested that senior management assist him in his workload. No action was taken. He then suffered a stress-induced breakdown. Afterwards, he was promised that the work pressure would be relieved if he returned to work. The plaintiff returned to work but the promised assistance never materialised and he suffered another breakdown.

Held: The defendant was liable for the recurrence of the stress-related illness. While the first breakdown may not have been foreseeable, the second one was and the employer was negligent in failing to take reasonable steps to prevent the recurrence of the illness. *Walker v Northumberland CC* [1995] 1 All E.R. 737.

Hatton v Sutherland [2002] 2 All E.R. 1 (CA)

Two of the plaintiffs were teachers in public sector schools (*Hatton* and *Barber*). The third was an administrator at a local training centre (*Jones*) and the fourth was an operative in a factory (*Bishop*). Each of these plaintiffs brought claims for stress-related illness against their employer.

Held: Only one of the claims was upheld by the Court of Appeal. However, the decision is important because the court set out a number of practical propositions in determining an employer's liability for occupational stress. These may be summarised as follows:

1. There are no special control requirements which must apply in such circumstances. Unlike nervous shock cases, the same fear of the floodgates does not apply.
2. Threshold question—was the kind of harm to this particular employee reasonably foreseeable? Reasonable fortitude cannot be expected in all cases—each employee must be treated differently.
3. Foreseeability will depend on what the employer knows, or ought reasonably to know, about the individual employee. An employer is entitled to assume that the employee can withstand the normal pressures of the job unless he knows of some particular problem or vulnerability.
4. The test is the same whatever the employment.
5. Questions which may influence reasonable foreseeability include: the nature and extent of the work, whether the workload is normal for this type of job. Are demands made of the employee unreasonable when compared to the demands made of others in the same or comparable job? Are there abnormal levels of sickness and absenteeism in the department? Are there signs from the employee that he is suffering from such stress?
6. The employer is entitled to take what the employee tells him at face value unless he has good reason to think to the contrary. No requirement to conduct searching enquiries.
7. To trigger a duty to take steps the indications of impending harm to health arising from the stress at work must be plain enough for any reasonable employer to realise that he should do something about it.
8. The employer is only liable where he has failed to take reasonable steps to handle the situation.
9. The size and scope of the employer's operation will be taken into consideration—the demands it places on fellow employees.
10. An employer can only reasonably be expected to take steps which are likely to do some good.
11. An employer who offers a professional counselling service is unlikely to be found liable for stress-related injury.

12. If the only reasonable step would be to dismiss the employee, the employer will not be found liable where he allows the employee to continue to work.
13. The steps the employer could/should have taken must be identified if the employer is to be found to have breached his duty.
14. Plaintiff must show that it was the breach of duty and not the stress itself which caused the injury.
15. Where the harm suffered comes from more than one cause, the employer should only pay for that proportion of the harm which is attributable to his wrongdoing.
16. Assessment of damages must take into consideration any pre-existing disorder.

In the case of *Jones* (the administrative assistant), the court found in favour of the plaintiff. She was off sick for a number of months with anxiety and depression. She was then made redundant. Prior to her absence on sick leave, there was no significant event which should have alerted her employers to the risk of a possible breakdown. Her employers were aware of the extra demands that were made of her in the workplace. They were aware of her complaints regarding the unreasonable behaviour of her manager—she had been threatened with the non-renewal of her post if she did not stop complaining about overwork. Her complaints were treated sufficiently seriously in that extra help was arranged, but never materialised. She also made two written complaints about how her workload in these circumstances was affecting her health. The failure to act and alleviate these problems—where the employer was aware of them—was sufficient to find them liable.

Commentary

The factors listed above are intended to provide general guidelines as to the potential liability of an employer for such injuries. In *Barber v Somerset CC* [2004] U.K.H.L. 13, an appeal from *Hatton*, the House of Lords generally approved of the principles laid out in *Hatton*. However, their Lordships did emphasise that such injury was a complex thing which could be brought about by a combination of different factors (such as personal life) and not just the job alone. Different people had different breaking points. Lord Walker in *Barber* also warned against relying too heavily on factor (6) of *Hatton* i.e. the employer is entitled to take what the employee tells him at face value, pointing out that the principles laid down in *Hatton* did not have statutory force and were only to be used as practical guidance. Lord Walker also pointed to the fact that some employees, particularly senior high level ones, would usually have strong inhibitions against complaining about overwork and stress, even if it became a threat to their health.

Cox has observed that in terms of general negligence principles, propositions (2) to (7) of *Hatton* should be classified as answering the question whether a duty of care is owed by the employer for such injury. Whether the standard of care has been breached will be answered by propositions (8) to (13). Propositions (14) to (15) go towards the question of causation and proposition (16) relates to the question of damage. (Cox, *Recent Developments in the Rules Relating to Workplace Stress: The Supreme Court Decision in Berber v Dunnes Stores*, Q.R.T.L., Vol 3, Issue 3, 2008/09 at 17). The *Hatton* principles were also approved as useful guidelines by Laffoy J. of the High Court in *McGrath v Trintech Technologies Ltd* [2004] I.E.H.C. 342.

Key Principle: An assessment of the existence of an employer's liability for workplace stress may now be summarized by the following questions: (1) Did the employee suffer recognizable psychiatric harm? (2) was that harm attributable to the workplace? and (3) was the harm foreseeable? (per Clarke J. in *Maher v Jabil Global Services Ltd* [2005] I.E.H.C. 130).

Maher v Jabil Global Services Ltd [2005]

The plaintiff complained that because of overwork he suffered from occupational stress. The plaintiff went on sick leave and following a medical examination by medical representatives of the employers it was recommended that he not return to work to the same job and pressures. He returned to a lighter level of work which he had been doing prior to his promotion. At this stage, the plaintiff then alleged that he suffered from stress because he was being underworked and alleged that the perception was that he had been demoted.

Held: Relying heavily on point (3) above, the court stated that the plaintiff failed to make out a claim in respect of either period of employment. The court accepted that during the first period of employment, the work set out for the plaintiff initially was not unduly burdensome (objectively speaking) and therefore the plaintiff's breakdown was not foreseeable. In the second period of his employment, the court stated that because the plaintiff had not made frequent complaints about his work situation his second breakdown was not something the employer should have foreseen. *Maher v Jabil Global Services Ltd* [2005] I.E.H.C. 130.

Key Principle: An employer will only be liable for the employee's stress-related illness where he or she has failed to take reasonable care.

Berber v Dunnes Stores Ltd [2009]

The respondent worked for 21 years with the appellant. He suffered from Crohn's disease since his teens and his employer (the appellant) was aware of his condition. In 2000, the respondent noticed a change in the management's attitude towards him. He did not travel on business as much and he noticed an increased interest from his employers in his health. He was subsequently transferred to another position within the company. In November 2000, following a dispute with his supervisor, the respondent was suspended with pay. On December 7, 2000, the appellant was informed via the respondent's solicitors that he was suffering from stress as a result of the incident. In late December 2000, the respondent reported for work having been medically cleared to do so. Upon his return to work, the respondent had another disagreement with his supervisor regarding his dress which was considered to be too casual. The respondent was absent from work four days later on stress-related grounds. The respondent alleged that his illness was exacerbated by the disagreements he had with his supervisor. In particular, he alleged that two issues during this time caused him upset: (1) a duty roster had been circulated by management for new trainees which had included his name; and (2) a personalized training plan had been set down for him. These incidents were upsetting to him as they were associated with new trainees and did not take into account of the fact that he was an employee of 21 years with the appellant. In May 2001, the respondent commenced legal proceedings against the appellant for inter alia personal injuries (in the form of workplace stress) caused by the behavior of his employer.

Held: The appellant was not liable. From receipt of the respondent's letter on December 7, 2000, the employer was actually aware that the respondent was suffering from stress and that that stress was affecting his Crohn's disease. However, the appellant was not found to have acted unreasonably. While the appellant had made a mistake in relation to the duty roster it was not foreseeable that this would cause the respondent to suffer a stress-related illness. Following discussions with the respondent, the appellant had corrected the error and had circulated the corrected version. While the circulation of the corrected version may have fallen short of that which was agreed between the parties it was not such a mistake as to make the injury foreseeable. As regards the contents of the training plan, the court held that the appellant's failure to discuss same with the respondent while he was on sick leave due to stress was not unreasonable. Indeed, the failure to discuss the training plan during this time was probably beneficial to the respondent in that if such a matter was a stressor it was best to leave the discussion until he was certified as medically fit to return to work. *Berber v Dunnes Stores Ltd* [2009] I.E.S.C. 10.

Corbett v Ireland [2006]

The plaintiff was a soldier who served in the Lebanon. A number of unrelated incidents caused him to suffer trauma. In the first, he witnessed an explosion which killed and mutilated a South Lebanese Army soldier. In the second, an Israeli soldier was killed in an explosion some 50 feet from the plaintiff's lookout post. In the third, a helicopter crashed killing all the occupants. This incident was not directly witnessed by the plaintiff. The plaintiff initiated proceedings against his employer for failing to take reasonable care for him when he was suffering from stress-related illness after the above incidents.
Held: The claim failed. The employer had acted reasonably in the circumstances. The plaintiff had been provided with comprehensive training prior to his departure to the Lebanon. After the first incident, his commanding officer had temporarily removed him from duty. Furthermore, the plaintiff had ample opportunity to bring any difficulties that he may have been experiencing to the attention of his employer and had failed to do so. Based on the above, there was no evidence that the employer was aware, nor should have been aware, of the plaintiff's injuries. *Corbett v Ireland*, High Court, April 25, 2006.

Key Principle: Notwithstanding the fact that the occurrence of the employee's stress-related illness may not have been foreseeable, an employer will be liable where he or she fails to act in a reasonable manner to alleviate the damage where it has occurred.

Murtagh v Minister for Defence [2008]

The plaintiff was a member of the Defence Forces. He volunteered for service in the Lebanon. Prior to commencing such service he submitted to a medical examination for which he received the top grade. While based in the Lebanon, the plaintiff and his colleagues came under heavy mortar and gun fire on a regular and prolonged basis. The plaintiff began to display signs of anxiety and was prescribed sedatives by the army physician. The plaintiff's suitability to serve was questioned and the physician advised that he was not to serve unless there were at least two colleagues present with him at all times. Despite this advice the plaintiff was allowed to return to active duty. Thereafter, witnesses testified that the plaintiff appeared "out of it" when the base came under fire and even during electrical storms the plaintiff would display signs of nervousness which was not considered normal. After his return to duty, a fellow soldier that he knew was killed. While the plaintiff did not witness the death, he did hear the firing and later learned of the death. Soon after this incident, another soldier who the plaintiff was friendly with was also killed. After these deaths, the plaintiff began displaying further signs of stress. The plaintiff alleged that his employer was liable for the stress-related injuries which he developed as a consequence.

Held: The defendant had failed in their duty of care to the plaintiff in the circumstances, not by his exposure to the explosions, the death of his colleagues or the other dangers which presented themselves in the course of his work as a soldier in the Lebanon, but because it had failed to observe or recognize the warning signs of the stress, failed to observe the manifestations of this stress while he was serving in the Lebanon and had negligently failed to obtain remedial therapy and treatment for the plaintiff after those symptoms presented themselves. *Murtagh v Minister for Defence* [2008] I.E.H.C. 292.

(iii) *Bullying and Harassment*

Key Principle: An employer has a duty to take reasonable care not to expose his or her employees to bullying and harassment in the workplace. If that duty is breached then the employer may be liable for the plaintiff's consequent injuries if it is proven that it was the employer's negligence which caused them.

Quigley v Complex Tooling & Moulding Ltd [2008]

The plaintiff alleged that he had been subjected to constant verbal harassment and bullying by his manager while at work. He was of the opinion that he was being constantly scrutinized and unfairly selected for criticism. He had been issued with a verbal warning which had not been removed from his file after a period of time (which would be normal in the case of other employees with similar warnings). When he discussed the matter with the human resources department he had a dispute with another member of staff where he used abusive language. He was given a final written warning in relation to the incident. Following an unofficial work stoppage which the plaintiff was involved (although there was no evidence that he organized it) he was dismissed. The plaintiff successfully brought an action for unfair dismissal against his employer. The plaintiff also brought a claim for personal injuries on the basis that his employer's negligence had caused him psychiatric harm.

Held: The defendant's claim failed on the issue of causation. The medical evidence was that the plaintiff had not visited his doctor until some fourteen months after his dismissal when he told the doctor that his depression had started six months previously. Thus, while the plaintiff's claims of bullying and harassment were upheld and his employer was in breach of the duty of care to him, there was no evidence of a causative link between the stress and the bullying and harassment. It was more likely that his injuries were caused by the stress of the dismissal proceedings which arose after he had been dismissed rather than by the bullying behavior which had occurred before he had been dismissed. *Quigley v Complex Tooling & Moulding Ltd* [2008] I.E.S.C. 44.

(iv) *Witnessing an injury to another employee*

Key Principle: An employer may be liable where, due to his or her negligence in failing to provide a safe system of work, an employee witnesses an injury to another causing that employee to suffer from a recognisable psychiatric illness.

Curran v Cadbury (Irl) Ltd [2000]

Some machinery broke down in the employee's workplace. The employer called a fitter to repair the machinery which was shut down as he examined it. The plaintiff was told—via hand signals through a Perspex partition—not to turn the machine on until the fitter was finished. She alleged that these instructions were not clear and she later turned the machine on at which point she became aware that the fitter was inside. She switched off the machine and ran down to the fitter who, as it happened, had been unhurt. The plaintiff claimed that she had suffered psychiatric trauma, due to her employer's negligence, as she had thought she had seriously injured the fitter.

Held: The defendant had failed to take reasonable care in the circumstances for the safety of its employees. The defendant had fallen short of what the reasonable employer should have done and the resulting damage was a foreseeable consequence of such failure. *Curran v Cadbury (Irl) Ltd* [2000] 2 I.L.R.M. 343.

(v) *Inherently dangerous work*

Key Principle: The duty of care to provide a safe system of work also applies to work which is inherently dangerous. In such circumstances, the employer is expected, notwithstanding the inherent dangerousness of the work, to take reasonable steps to ensure the safety of his or her employees.

Walsh v Securicor (Ireland) Ltd [1993]

The plaintiff was employed as a security guard in a van for the defendant company. The van was robbed and the plaintiff was struck over the head. The plaintiff brought an action against his employer alleging that his negligent failure to have a safe system of work in place caused his injuries by facilitating the attack.

Held: The court found in favour of the plaintiff, laying particular emphasis on the fact that the defendant had not changed the route taken by the van in seven years. As Egan J. stated: "this was a high risk operation and the defendant was bound to avail of every safety precaution, not just the provision of a Garda escort." *Walsh v Securicor (Ireland) Ltd* [1993] 2 I.R. 507.

12. VICARIOUS LIABILITY

INTRODUCTION

The doctrine of vicarious liability is as a loss distribution mechanism developed by the law of torts. The doctrine provides that, in certain circumstances, the defendant may be held strictly liable for the wrongdoing of another which caused injury to a third party. As a strict form of tortious liability, the doctrine is only applied in limited circumstances. It is most commonly applied where the wrongdoer is an employee of another party (the employer), and that employee commits the wrong while acting in the *scope* or *course* of his or her employment. In the words of Lord in *Staveley Iron and Chemical Co v Jones* [1956] A.C. 627, "It is a rule of law that an employer, though guilty of no fault himself, is liable for damage done by the fault or negligence of his servant acting in the course of his employment." An employee is said to be engaged under a "contract of service" and an independent contractor is engaged under a "contract for services."

Justifications for imposing vicarious liability

Because it is an exceptional form of liability which essentially places blame on an employer who is not at fault (in the traditional legal sense) the imposition of vicarious liability has given rise to much debate as to the underlying rationale for its application. Fleming has observed that the doctrine represents "a compromise between two conflicting policies: on the one hand, the social interest in furnishing an innocent tort victim with recourse against a financially responsible defendant; on the other, a hesitation to foist any undue burden on business enterprise" (Fleming, *The Law of Torts*, 9th edn, (LBC Services, 1998) at 409–410).

Its application has also been justified on the basis that as the employer was in control of the employee's actions—in that the employer was in a position of authority or responsibility over the employee—then the employer should be made vicariously liable for that employee's wrongful actions (*Moynihan v Moynihan* [1975] I.R. 192 (SC)). Another justification is that because the employee would not have been in a position to commit the wrong but for his or her employer's activities, it is only fair that the employer should be made liable, as "the master set the whole thing in motion" (*Hutchinson v The York, Newcastle and Berwick Railway Co* (1850) 5 Exch. 343 at 350). Yet another justification is that the doctrine acts as a loss distribution mechanism. The loss is shifted, in economic terms, from the wrongdoer to another party who is usually in a better position to absorb the loss (the employer). This is also known as the "deep pockets" theory.

1. EMPLOYEE V INDEPENDENT CONTRACTOR

Because vicarious liability does not generally arise in cases involving independent contractors but more usually in the case of employees, the question as to who is or is not an employee is critical.

Key Principle: In determining whether the relationship between the parties is one of employer/employee, the extent of the control exercised by the employer over the worker's activities is of crucial importance.

Walshe v Baileboro Co-op Agricultural and Dairy Society and Gargan [1939]

The plaintiff was injured when struck by a horse and cart driven by Gargan on behalf of the Co-op. The horse and cart belonged to Gargan and he was paid in a piecework fashion.
Held: While Gargan provided his own equipment and was paid based on his effectiveness in completing the work, the court found that the Co-op was vicariously liable for the plaintiff's injuries. While the court considered the factors already outlined to be relevant, it found that as the Co-op controlled the hours of collection of the milk and Gargan was left with little discretion as to how it was to be done, the extent of the Co-op's control justified the imposition of liability on the shoulders of the first defendant. *Walshe v Baileboro Co-op Agricultural and Dairy Society and Gargan* [1939] Ir. Jur. Rep. 77 (HC).

Phelan v Coillte Teoranta [1993]

C worked for the defendant repairing broken machinery. He was paid an hourly rate, mileage expenses, was not entitled to any holiday pay, used his own tools and dealt with his own tax affairs. He reported to various sites as and when required by the defendant. The plaintiff, an employee of the defendant, was injured by the negligence of C and brought an action in negligence against the defendant on the basis of the doctrine of vicarious liability.

Held: The control exercised by the defendant over C was akin to that of master and servant. In such circumstances, the court was willing to impose vicarious liability on the defendant. *Phelan v Coillte Teoranta* [1993] 1 I.R. 18 (HC).

O'Keeffe v Hickey [2008]

The appellant was a pupil at a National School. The first-named defendant was a school teacher and principal at the school. The first-named defendant provided music lessons to the appellant that took place in the classroom either during the play-break or in the afternoons after school. The first-named defendant used these occasions to sexually abuse the appellant. The school was a Catholic School in the diocese of Cork and Ross. The manager of the school was a Canon Strich, but it appeared that due to an infirmity he was unable to carry out his duties and the de facto manager of the school was a Fr O'Ceallaigh. A number of complaints were made regarding the first named defendant by other parents. Following a number of meetings arranged by Fr O'Ceallaigh, the first-named defendant resigned. He later took up a position as a teacher in another school. As manager, Fr O'Ceallaigh wrote to the Department of Education and informed it that the first named defendant had resigned (although the letter did not state why) and that he planned to appoint another teacher in his place. In her action against the first-named defendant, the appellant claimed that the Department of Education was the teacher's employer and was therefore vicariously liable for the actions of the first named defendant in the circumstances.

Held: The majority of the Supreme Court held that the Department of Education was not responsible on the basis that the teacher was not an employee of the Department and that, regardless, his actions were outside the course of his employment. In his judgment, Fennelly J. focused on the tripartite relationship between the teacher, the school (through its manager) and the State. Fennelly J. concluded that while the Department had the ultimate power to withdraw recognition of the teacher's qualifications (thereby prohibiting him from teaching in any school) the actual contract of employment was with the manager of the school. Responsibility for day-to-day management remained with the school manager. *O'Keeffe v Hickey* [2008] I.E.S.C. 72.

Key Principle: While the control test will be applied in a liberal fashion, the court will not make a finding that is totally at odds with the actual nature of the relationship.

Carroll v Post National Lottery [1996]

The plaintiff argued that the Lotto agents of the defendant company should be considered employees of that company for the purposes of vicarious liability. The agents were given training by the defendant company in the operation of the Lotto terminals, however, the agents were in receipt of a sales commission from the defendant company.

Held: The court found that the mere fact that the agents received training in the operation of the terminals was insufficient to fix the defendant company with vicarious liability. To hold otherwise, in the words of Costello P., would be to do violence to the well established characteristics of that relationship. *Carroll v Post National Lottery* High Court, (Costello P.), April 17, 1996.

2. THE SCOPE / COURSE OF EMPLOYMENT

Introduction

Even if the wrongdoer has been proven to be an employee of the defendant, vicarious liability will only apply where it can also be established that the employee was acting within the scope or course of his or her employment at the time they caused the injury. The scope or course of employment tests have been used interchangeably by the courts when assessing whether the employee's actions impose liability on the shoulders of the employer. The authorities would appear to conflict with each other in this area and it can be difficult to predict the outcome in any given case as to whether the employee was acting within the scope or course of employment.

The Scope of Employment / Implied Authority Test

Key Principle: An employee will be said to have been acting within the scope of his or her employment where the employer has authorized his or her actions. This authority may be expressed or implied.

Poland v Parr & Sons [1927]

An employee struck a child because he reasonably believed that the child was stealing his employer's property.
Held: The employee had the authority to act in defence of his employer's property in emergency circumstances. His actions while not advisable could be considered to be within his delegated authority and therefore his employer was liable. *Poland v Parr & Sons* [1927] 1 K.B. 236.

Lloyd v Grace, Smith & Co [1912]

The employee was a clerk who was authorised to handle clients' title deeds and complete conveyances. The employee fraudulently conveyed a client's property to himself.
Held: The firm was vicariously liable for the employee's actions. The court stated that it was reasonable for the client to rely on the clerk's authority to do what he told her to do. The employer had effectively given the impression that the employee had delegated authority to so act and, therefore, the employee was found to be acting within the scope of his employment. *Lloyd v Grace, Smith & Co* [1912] A.C. 716.

Key Principle: It is not sufficient for the plaintiff to establish that the acts were done within the employee's delegated authority, those acts must also be done *for* the employer.

Farry v GN Rly Co [1898]

The plaintiff was a passenger on a train journey when a dispute arose with a station employee as to whether the plaintiff had the appropriate ticket to travel. The employee detained the plaintiff forcing him to give up his ticket.
Held: The defendant company was vicariously liable in tort for false imprisonment as a result of the employee's actions. The court held that in order to ground liability in such circumstances it was necessary to assess first, whether the act done was within the normal scope of the employee's authority i.e. ensuring that all who were travelling on the train had the appropriate ticket and secondly, whether the act was done by the employee for the purpose of his or her employment or whether

the act was done for personal spite or vengeance. In the circumstances, the employee's wrong was committed within the scope of his employment and it was done, however misguidedly, for his employer's benefit. *Farry v GN Rly Co* [1898] 2 I.R. 352.

The Course of Employment Test

Introduction

The course of employment test is a more liberal test than the scope of employment test and takes into consideration the practical realities of the modern workplace. The test is said to derive from a formulation outlined by Salmond in his textbook (*Salmond and Heuston on the Law of Torts*, 19th edn (1987) at 521–522) which provides that:

> "[A] master is responsible not merely for what he authorises his servant to do, but also for the way in which he does it. If a servant does negligently that which he was authorised to do carefully, or if he does fraudulently that which he was authorised to do honestly, or if he does mistakenly that which he was authorised to correctly, his master will answer for that negligence, fraud or mistake.
>
> On the other hand, if the unauthorised and wrongful act of the servant is not so connected with the authorised act as to be a mode of doing it, but is an independent act, the master is not responsible: for in such a case the servant is not acting in the course of his employment, but has gone outside of it."

The course of employment test as set down by Salmond is more flexible than the scope of employment test as it may apply not only to wrongs authorized by the employer but also wrongs not so authorized but which are connected with the employment.

Key Principle: An employee will be acting in the course of employment where he or she is not only doing what he or she was employed to do but it also applies where he or she is doing anything which is considered to be reasonably incidental to that employment (per Lord Goff, *Smith v Stages* [1989] 1 All E.R. 833 at 836).

Kay v ITW [1968]

The employee was employed as fork lift driver. While driving a fork lift at work his route to the entrance of a warehouse was blocked by a lorry. The employee decided to move the lorry out of his way in order that he could continue his work. He injured another while reversing the lorry. **Held:** The employee was acting within the course of his employment. Ultimately, the employee was trying to do his job at the time of the accident, even if he was not authorized to drive the lorry. *Kay v ITW* [1968] 1 Q.B. 140.

Poland v John Parr & Sons [1927]

The defendant's employee hit the plaintiff with his hand as he believed that the plaintiff was stealing the employer's property and was trying to prevent the theft.
Held: The employee's conduct was within the course of his employment. The behavior was not so extreme as to be unconnected with the work and while perhaps not the most advisable way of protecting his employer's property was considered to be an act which was within the course of his employment. *Poland v John Parr & Sons* [1927] 1 K.B. 236.

Key Principle: The time and place the injury occurred will be relevant to determining whether the employee's actions are considered to have been committed during the course of his or her employment.

Boyle v Ferguson [1911]

A car salesman was driving in a car accompanied by two women at 7 pm on a Saturday evening when he was involved in an accident.
Held: The salesman was found to be acting within the course of his employment at the time of the accident. The court paid particular regard to the fact that his hours of work were quite flexible, his employer was paying for the petrol at the time and he was, by travelling with the women in the car, creating the impression expected of a good car salesman. *Boyle v Ferguson* [1911] 2 I.R. 489.

Smith v Stages [1989]

The defendant sent two of his employees to work on a project some distance away. In addition to their normal pay, the employees were paid travelling expenses. The employees finished their work early and on their journey home were involved in a car accident. The employee driving the car was uninsured and the plaintiff sued the defendant under the principle of vicarious liability.

Held: The employee driver was acting within the course of his employment when the accident occurred, even though he was travelling home at the time. The court found that as he was being paid travelling expenses, he was on his employer's time and was still working for the purposes of vicarious liability. *Smith v Stages* [1989] A.C. 928.

Key Principle: The course of employment test provides that an employer will not only be held liable for the acts of his or her employee but also for the manner in which he or she does those acts.

Century Insurance Co Ltd v Northern Ireland Road Transport Board [1942]

The employee was a petrol lorry driver who, while transferring petrol from a tanker to the tank lit a cigarette and threw away the lighted match he had used to light the cigarette. As a consequence, there was an explosion as the match ignited and the resulting fire caused extensive damage.

Held: The lighting of the cigarette and the throwing away of the lighted match was an improper way of doing his work which involved the safe transfer and delivery of the petrol. The driver was found to be acting within the course of his employment. *Century Insurance Co Ltd v Northern Ireland Road* [1942] A.C. 509.

Limpus v London General Omnibus Co [1862]

A bus driver, in contravention of his employer's instructions, raced a bus he was driving and caused a collision.

Held: The employer was held vicariously liable for the driver's actions. While racing the bus was contrary to his employer's instructions, he was still doing his job (driving a bus) at the time of the collision. His actions were simply an unauthorized mode of doing something authorized by his employer. *Limpus v London General Omnibus Co* (1862) 1 H & C 526; 158 E.R. 993.

Gracey v Belfast Tramway Co [1901]

The defendant's employees were ordered to bring the defendant's horses to the forge in order to be shod. On their way to the forge, the employees raced each other on the horses, causing the plaintiff to be injured.

Held: The employees had acted negligently, but they had done so while carrying out their duties as employees of the defendant. Thus, the defendant was found vicariously liable for the plaintiff's injuries. *Gracey v Belfast Tramway Co* [1901] 2 I.R. 322.

Key Principle: An employer can be made vicariously liable for the intentional wrongs committed by an employee provided that there is a "sufficient connection" between the wrongdoing and the employee's employment.

Lister v Lesley Hall [2002]

The claimants were residents in a boarding school which was owned by the defendant. The defendant employed a warden whose responsibilities included supervising the boys, disciplining them and ensuring that they went to bed each evening and got up each morning. The warden sexually abused some of the schoolboys who sued the defendant on the basis that it was vicariously liable for the wrongful acts.

Held: The defendant was vicariously liable and the House of Lords reiterated the principle that providing the employee with an opportunity to commit the wrong does not itself make the employer vicariously liable—there must also be a sufficient connection between the employment and the wrong. Lord Hobhouse held that in order to establish whether a sufficient connection exists one had to first identify the duty owed by the employee to the employer which was breached and then identify the connection between that breach and the contractual duties owed by the employee to the employer. In this case, the defendant had a duty to protect and care for the children attending the school. The warden was engaged to assist the defendant in that duty. Instead, he acted in breach of his contractual duties by sexually abusing some of the schoolchildren entrusted to his care. There was a sufficient connection between the breach and the work. *Lister v Lesley Hall* [2002] 1 A.C. 215.

Delahunty v South Eastern Health Board [2003]

The plaintiff was a young boy who visited a friend in an industrial school and was sexually assaulted by a house parent at that institution. He claimed that the school and the Minister for Education and Science should be made vicariously liable for the acts of the employee.

Held: There was an absence of a strong connection between the perpetrator's employment and the wrong. The victim was a visitor to the school in respect of whom the perpetrator had no particular duties quite unlike *Lister* where the perpetrator, as part of his employment duties, had a close relationship with the victims. The High Court also stated that the Minister for Education and Science could not be held vicariously liable as the connection between the Minister and the plaintiff was "quite remote." *Delahunty v South Eastern Health Board* [2003] I.R. 361.

O'Keeffe v Hickey [2008]

The appellant was a pupil at a National School. The first named defendant was school teacher and principal at the school. The first named defendant provided music lessons to the appellant that took place in the classroom either during the play-break or in the afternoons after school. The first-named defendant used these occasions to sexually abuse the appellant. In her action against the first named defendant, the appellant claimed that the Department of Education was the teacher's employer and was therefore vicariously liable for the actions of the first-named defendant in the circumstances.

Held: While the majority of the Supreme Court held that the Department of Education should not be held vicariously liable for the sexual abuse by the teacher it was on the basis that the teacher was not considered an employee. The court was very much divided on the issue as to whether the teacher's actions could be considered to be within the course of employment. Hardiman J. in particular did not favour a finding that the actions of the teacher fell within the course of his employment. He adopted a narrow view of the test and held that such acts could never be considered to be so closely connected to the teacher's employment as to be a mode of doing the work. Both Geoghegan J. and Fennelly J. on the other hand expressed support for the proposition that under certain circumstances, acts of sexual abuse by a school-teacher could be considered to be acts which are committed during the course of employment. *O'Keeffe v Hickey* [2008] I.E.S.C. 72.

Reilly v Devereux [2009]

The plaintiff was employed as a member of the Defence Forces. He complained that he had been sexually assaulted on a number of occasions during the course of his employment by the first named defendant who was a Sergeant Major in the Army and the plaintiff's superior officer.

Held: The defendant was not vicariously liable. The relationship between the plaintiff and his abuser, while of a supervisory nature, was not an intimate one unlike that in *Lister* and therefore there was not a sufficient connection which could justify the imposition of vicarious liability. *Reilly v Devereux* [2009] I.E.S.C. 22.

Key Principle: The employer will not be made vicariously liable where the employee has acted outside the scope/course of his or her employment. In other words, if the conduct in question is completely unconnected with the employee's employment then vicarious liability will not arise.

Storey v Ashton [1869]

The defendant employed a driver to make deliveries. The employee was involved in an accident while at work when he embarked on a detour in order to visit his brother-in-law.

Held: The employer was not vicariously liable in these circumstances. The employee was involved in an activity which was so totally unconnected with his employment he was considered to be on a "frolic of his own" and consequently the employer was not vicariously liable. *Storey v Ashton* [1869] LR 4 Q.B. 476.

O'Connell v Bateman [1932]

An employee borrowed his employer's vehicle in order to visit his parents after work. The employee was involved in an accident while driving the vehicle.

Held: The court found that the employee was not acting in the course of his employment when the accident occurred. While he was driving his employer's vehicle with his permission, his journey was wholly unconnected with his employment. *O Connell v Bateman* [1932] LJ Ir 160.

13. TRESPASS TO THE PERSON

The tort of trespass to the person is actionable per se (without proof of damage), this is so because the courts regard the protection of bodily protection as being so important that it must be protected even where no actual damage has resulted. It is significant that where actual bodily injury has occurred as a result of the trespass, the defendant will be liable for all the direct consequences (mental and physical) of his or her act without recourse to artificial limitations that are applied to the recovery of such losses in actions involving negligence. With the personal security of the individual to the forefront of its mind, the law has developed the following specific torts: (1) Battery (2) Assault (3) False Imprisonment (4) Intentional Infliction of Emotional Distress.

Key Principle: A trespass is committed where the defendant through his or her voluntary actions directly (whether intentionally or negligently) interferes with the person of the plaintiff.

Scott v Shepherd [1773]

In that case, the defendant threw fireworks into a busy market-place. X panicked and threw the fireworks away. They landed close to Y who also picked them up and tossed them away and thereby struck the plaintiff. The plaintiff brought an action against the defendant in trespass to the person.
Held: The injury to the plaintiff was caused by the defendant, notwithstanding the actions of X and Y. The defendant's initial action was held to amount to direct interference for the purposes of the tort. Further, the actions of X and Y did not amount to trespass as their actions were not voluntary, but motivated by self-preservation. *Scott v Shepherd* (1773) 96 E.R. 525.

1. BATTERY

Key Principle: A person commits a battery where he or she applies direct force to the person of another without that person's consent.

Humphries v Connor [1864]

A police officer removed an orange lily from the plaintiff's coat in order to preserve the public peace in circumstances where the wearing of the lily could be interpreted as incitement to a nearby crowd.

Held: While the court was satisfied that the policeman's actions could amount to a battery, it held that the actions were defensible as they were deemed necessary in order to preserve the peace. *Humphries v Connor* (1864) 17 Ir C.L.R. 1 (Q.B.).

Key Principle: Not all touching will amount to a battery. It must be of a kind that is unwanted by the plaintiff and which is considered unacceptable by society.

Collins v Wilcock [1984]

A female police officer attempted to question a woman whom she suspected of committing an offence. While in the process of cautioning her, the police officer grabbed hold of the woman's arm in order to detain her.

Held: The police officer had acted outside her powers in grabbing the woman's arm in circumstances where she was not arresting her. Her conduct amounted to a battery. *Collins v Wilcock* [1984] 3 All E.R. 374.

F v West Berkshire Health Authority [1990]

F was a 36-year-old female patient with the mental capacity of a very young child. She had begun a sexual relationship with another patient. Psychiatric evidence was heard to the effect that a pregnancy could have a devastating effect on F and it was the accepted medical opinion that sterilisation would be the best course available to ensure that she did not become pregnant. F's mother sought, as against the health authority, a declaration that the absence of F's consent would not make the sterilisation an unlawful act amounting to a battery.

Held: The House of Lords rejected the view in *Wilson v Pringle* [1986] 2 All E.R. 1006 that in order for touching to be considered a battery it must be of a hostile nature. While granting F's mother's request based on medical necessity, the House of Lords did reiterate the common law view that the tort protects the individual's right to bodily integrity. Thus, the touching of a person by a surgeon during the course of surgery, for example, may not be characterised as hostile, but where the consent of the patient was lacking, it could amount to a battery under tort law. *F v West Berkshire Health Authority* [1990] 2 A.C. 1.

Key Principle: The touching must be intentional in the sense that it is a voluntary act. However, it is not necessary that the plaintiff prove that the defendant intended to injure the plaintiff.

Nash v Sheehan [1953]

The plaintiff requested a permanent wave from the defendant hairdresser. Instead, she received a tone rinse which produced a negative skin reaction.
Held: The application of a tone rinse was a very different procedure to that which the plaintiff had requested and as such it could not have been said that she had consented to it. The application of the tone rinse in such circumstances amounted to a battery. *Nash v Sheehan* [1955] C.L.Y. 3726

Key Principle: The intention to commit the act of battery need not exist at the commencement of the act, provided it is formed while the act is still continuing.

Fagan v Commissioner of Metropolitan Police [1969]

The defendant unintentionally stopped his car on a policeman's foot. When asked to move the vehicle he deliberately delayed before doing so.
Held: The delay in moving the vehicle constituted a battery. The later intention to inflict unlawful force was a battery as it was directed towards a continuing act. *Fagan v Commissioner of Metropolitan Police* [1969] 1 Q.B. 439

2. ASSAULT

Key Principle: An assault is committed where one party indicates to another that he or she is about to inflict unlawful force on that person and the person who is subject of the threat reasonably believes that he or she will do so.

Stephens v Myers [1830]

During a parish meeting, it was decided by a majority of those present that the defendant should be ejected from the proceedings. The defendant approached the plaintiff with clenched fists declaring that he would rather pull the plaintiff from his chair than leave the meeting. As he approached the plaintiff he was prevented from advancing any further by another person present at the meeting.
Held: While the defendant was stopped short of the plaintiff and prevented from striking him, it was held that because the defendant's actions caused the plaintiff to reasonably believe that a battery was about to be perpetrated against him, then an assault had been committed. *Stephens v Myers* (1830) 4 C&P 349, 172 E.R. 735.

Key Principle: To be actionable as an assault, it must be established that the plaintiff *reasonably* apprehended the commission of an *immediate* battery.

Tuberville v Savage [1669]

The plaintiff and defendant were involved in an argument. At one point, the defendant placed his hand on his sword and said, "If it were not assize time (peacetime), I would not take such language from you."
Held: The defendant's conduct did not amount to an assault. While the action of placing his hand on his sword in a threatening manner during the argument could have amounted to an assault, the fact that it was accompanied by words which negatived the perceived threat meant that a reasonable person in all the circumstances would not have formed the view that an immediate battery was about to committed. *Tuberville v Savage* (1669) 1 Mod. Rep. 3.

Thomas v N.U.M. [1985]

During a strike at a coal mine, picketers jeered and made threatening gestures towards working miners who were being transported to the colliery in a bus which was surrounded by a police cordon.
Held: The conduct of the picketers did not amount to an assault. The gestures made towards the working miners could not give rise to the apprehension of the commission of an immediate battery as the gestures were made towards workers who were on a bus and protected by police officers. *Thomas v N.U.M.* [1985] 2 All E.R. 1.

Key Principle: If the apprehension of physical contact was reasonably held, then it does not matter if that apprehension was mistakenly held.

R. v St George [1840]

The defendant pointed a gun at another who was unaware that the gun was not loaded.

Held: The defendant was liable for assault. The test to be applied was whether the victim reasonably believed that an assault was about to be immediately committed against his or her person. The fact that the application of force through use of the gun was impossible was irrelevant. The victim was not aware that the gun was unloaded. *R. v St George* (1840) 173 E.R. 921.

Key Principle: An assault cannot be committed if the victim is unaware of the threat of physical contact.

McCraney v Flanagan [1980]

The plaintiff alleged that the defendant has assaulted her by having sexual intercourse with her without her consent. Due to her intoxicated state, the plaintiff could not remember having sexual intercourse with the defendant but the medical evidence indicated that sexual intercourse had indeed taken place between the parties.

Held: The defendant was not guilty of assault in the circumstances. Because the key element of the tort is a mental one of apprehension of contact, it follows that the plaintiff must be aware of the defendant's actions at the time. *McCraney v Flanagan* (1980) 267 SE 2d 404.

Key Principle: Words uttered in a vacuum cannot constitute an assault. However, where words are said in a certain context, they may give rise to an action.

Read v Coker [1853]

The defendant employer, accompanied by other workmen, advanced on the plaintiff in a threatening manner and advised the plaintiff to leave the premises or he would "ring his neck" .

Held: It was found that the words said could amount to an assault in light of the surrounding circumstances. Where the words were said in circumstances where the defendant was accompanied by others when approaching the plaintiff in a menacing manner they amounted to an assault as an ordinary person would reasonably conclude, in those circumstances, that the words were a declaration of intent. *Read v Coker* (1853) 73 C.B. 850, [1853] 138 E.R. 1437.

3. FALSE IMPRISONMENT

Key Principle: False imprisonment is committed where the liberty of another is unlawfully restrained thereby depriving that person's freedom of movement totally.

Bird v Jones (1845)

The defendant attempted to cross a bridge which was partially cordoned off due to a regatta which was being held on the river. Officials halted his progress and informed him that he could cross the bridge at another point. **Held:** There was no false imprisonment, the restraint on liberty must be absolute. The plaintiff had the option to cross the bridge safely elsewhere. *Bird v Jones* (1845) 7 Q.B. 742.

Key Principle: The false imprisonment may be psychological. If the defendant causes the plaintiff to reasonably believe, whether by physical contact or by apparent authority, that his or her liberty to move is restricted then an action for false imprisonment may exist.

Phillips v GN Railway Co Ltd [1903]

An employee of the defendant company wrongly suspected a passenger on the defendant's train of travelling without the proper ticket. On arrival at her destination she was told by a ticket collector not to move. The plaintiff ordered a cab and told the driver to leave, however he refused to do so until the arrival of the stationmaster. A discussion took place which ended with the plaintiff getting into the cab and ordering the driver to move on.
Held: The court found that while her departure may have been delayed, there was no false imprisonment. The evidence indicated that the plaintiff was of a strong character and had not succumbed to the will of the defendant's employee to the extent that she felt that her liberty was totally restrained. *Phillips v GN Railway Co Ltd* (1903) 4 NIJR 154 (KBD).

Key Principle: False imprisonment may be committed even in circumstances where the plaintiff is not aware of his or her confinement. It should be noted however that in such circumstances the plaintiff could only expect to be awarded nominal damages.

Meering v Grahame-White Aviation Co Ltd **[1919]**

An employee of the defendant company had been suspected of theft. As part of the investigation, the employee was brought to a room for questioning. Unknown to him there were two security guards present outside the room who would have prevented his departure should he have chosen to leave.

Held: The defendant was liable for false imprisonment. The court was of the view that from the moment he came under the influence of the police the impression created was that he was no longer free to move as he pleased. *Meering v Grahame-White Aviation Co Ltd* [1919] 122 L.T. 44.

4. INTENTIONAL INFLICTION OF EMOTIONAL DISTRESS

Key Principle: An action in trespass to the person may exist where an individual intentionally or recklessly inflicts emotional suffering or distress on another.

Wilkinson v Downtown **[1897]**

The defendant played a practical joke on the plaintiff by arriving at her house and telling her that her husband was badly injured and that he required her presence. The shock caused by this news led to the plaintiff suffering mental distress which led to permanent physical damage.

Held: Notwithstanding the fact that the defendant did not intend to cause the injuries it was sufficient that he had acted recklessly and he was fixed with liability on the basis that his actions were willfully done (although the consequences may have not been intended). *Wilkinson v Downtown* [1897] 2 Q.B. 57.

Janiver v Sweeney **[1919]**

The plaintiff worked as a maid when a man called to the house claiming to be from Scotland Yard. He accused her of corresponding with a German spy. It transpired that the man was a private detective who was hoping to frighten her into handing him private letters in the possession of her employer.

Held: The plaintiff was entitled to recover damages for trespass as a consequence of the mental anguish (culminating in a physical illness) she suffered as a result of the man's impersonation. *Janiver v Sweeney* [1919] 2 K.B. 316 (C.A.).

DEFENCES TO TRESPASS TO THE PERSON

1. Self-Defence

Key Principle: The defendant must show that he or she reasonably believed that he or she needed to defend himself or herself and also that the force used was reasonable in all the circumstances.

Gregan v O Sullivan [1937]

The plaintiff, a 65 year old man, struck the defendant on the lip. In response, the younger man stabbed the plaintiff 13 times with a pitch-fork and broke his arm.

Held: The response of the defendant in these circumstances was unreasonable and disproportionate, with Byrne J. commenting that "steam hammers ought not to be used crush flies." *Gregan v O Sullivan* [1937] Ir. Jur. Rep. 64.

Lane v Holloway [1968]

The plaintiff had an argument with his next door neighbour eventually telling her "shut up, you monkey faced tart." At that point, her husband confronted the plaintiff and subsequently struck him a blow to the face which caused him to require 19 stitches.

Held: The response of the defendant to the plaintiff's provocation was disproportionate and he was liable in battery. *Lane v Holloway* [1968] 1 Q.B. 379.

2. Consent

Key Principle: Where an individual consents to the trespass, no action may be subsequently taken in trepass.

Hegarty v Shine [1878]

The plaintiff contracted a venereal disease as the result of having sexual intercourse with the defendant. The plaintiff was unaware that the defendant had such a disease.

Held: The plaintiff's action in battery was unsuccessful, as she had consented to the direct physical contact, i.e. the sexual intercourse, which had the collateral effect of causing her to contract the unwanted disease. *Hegarty v Shine* (1878) 4 L.R. Ir. 288.

Note: this decision has most likely been overruled by the recent English decision of *R v Dica* [2004] Q.B. 1257 (CA); where it was held that a person who knows they are infected by the HIV virus and have consensual, unprotected sexual intercourse with another may be guilty of criminal assault.

Key Principle: Consent to trespass to the person may be implied.

Simms v Leigh Rugby Football Club [1969]

The plaintiff was playing a rugby match when he was tackled and broke his leg.

Held: The plaintiff's claim for battery failed. The plaintiff had consented to running the risk of injury inherent in the sport. *Simms v Leigh Rugby Football Club* [1969] 2 All E.R. 923.

Key Principle: The conduct of the defendant must not exceed the bounds of the consent.

Corcoran v W & R Jacobs [1945]

As part of his contract of employment, the plaintiff had expressly agreed that the security personnel of the defendant could search him in certain circumstances, during his employment. In attempting to carry out a search of his person, a security guard aggressively searched his person.

Held: The security guard in acting in this manner had acted beyond the bounds of consent granted by the plaintiff as part of his contract of employment and as such the security guard's conduct amounted to a battery. *Corcoran v W & R Jacobs* [1945] I.R. 446.

R. v Billinghurst [1978]

During a match a rugby player was deliberately punched in the face by an opponent during an "off the ball" incident.

Held: The conduct of the opposing player amounted to a battery. While rugby players implicitly consent to force of the kind which could reasonably be expected to occur during a game, this consent does not extend to foul play beyond what is reasonable to expect under the rules of the game. *R. v Billinghurst* [1978] Crim. L.R. 553.

3. Necessity

Key Principle: An individual will not be liable in trespass where he or she can establish that his or her conduct was necessary to protect the health or safety of the plaintiff.

Leigh v Gladstone [1909]

The plaintiff was a prisoner who went on hunger strike. She was force fed by prison staff. She brought an action in trespass against the prison authorities.

Held: Her action in trespass failed. The court found that the prison authorities were forced to intervene and were under a duty to preserve the life and health of the prisoners in their custody. *Leigh v Gladstone* (1909) 26 T.L.R. 130.

4. Lawful Authority

Key Principle: The law permits certain individuals to commit what would otherwise be a trespass where they are authorised to do so under statute.

Humphries v Connor [1864]

A police officer removed an orange lily from the plaintiff's coat in order to preserve the public peace in circumstances where the wearing of the lily could be interpreted as incitement to a nearby crowd.

Held: While the court was satisfied that the policeman's actions could amount to a battery, it held that the actions were defensible in order to preserve the peace. *Humphries v Connor* (1864) 17 Ir C.L.R. 1 (Q.B.).

14. TRESPASS TO LAND

INTRODUCTION

A person is guilty of trespass to land where he or she intentionally or negligently enters or remains on, or brings something into contact with land in the possession of another. Such conduct will be actionable in tort unless there is lawful justification for doing so. Thus, the tort involves the direct interference with another's land without proper justification. The tort reinforces the Constitutional protection conferred by Art.40.5 which provides that the dwelling of every citizen is inviolable and shall not be forcibly entered save in accordance with law.

As with all forms of trespass, the tort is actionable per se and as such every invasion of property, be it ever so minute, is a trespass. (*Entick v Carrington* (1765) 2 Wils. K. B. 275 (English case)). See: *Wilcox v Kettel* [1937] 1 All E.R. 222 where an intrusion of 50 centimetres by a concrete foundation was held to be a trespass.

Key Principle: The tort protects an individual's right to possession of the land. Thus, the plaintiff must establish that he or she was in possession of the land when the interference occurred.

Whelan v Madigan [1978]

The defendant rented a number of flats to the plaintiffs. He sent a letter to the plaintiffs stating that he intended to enter and inspect the premises. The defendant arrived at the said date and as he did not have a key to the main door of the complex he forced the door open with a screwdriver. During his visit he caused damage to the plaintiff's partition walls and removed chairs from another tenant's landing. The plaintiffs sought damages inter alia for trespass.

Held: Notwithstanding the fact that the tenants were not the legal owners of the property, they were in rightful occupation and were able to successfully pursue an action in trespass to land against the defendant landlord. *Whelan v Madigan* [1978] I.L.R.M. 136.

Key Principle: It is no defence for the trespasser to plead that another had a better right to possession. This is known as the principle of *jus tertii*.

Petrie v Owners of SS Rostrevor [1898]

The plaintiff had used an area of foreshore as an oyster bed. The plaintiff brought an action in trespass against the defendant when he damaged the bed while trying to remove his ship that had run aground on the foreshore. Legal title over the foreshore rested with the State and not the plaintiff. The defendant argued that as the plaintiff did not possess legal title in the property the plaintiff could not bring an action for trespass.

Held: The court agreed that the plaintiff was in physical possession of the foreshore and was consequently in legal possession as against the world except its true owner. However, the plaintiff's action was ultimately unsuccessful as the defendant had received the permission of the true legal owners of the foreshore before attempting to remove their ship. *Petrie v Owners of SS Rostrevor* [1898] 2 I.R. 556.

Key Principle: A person who initially enters property legally or with consent may lose that entitlement if he or she subsequently abuses that right of entry.

Webb v Ireland [1988]

The plaintiffs lawfully entered property for the ostensible purpose of viewing a national monument. However, upon entry they dug up the earth in search of treasure trove.

Held: The plaintiffs became trespassers ab initio from the moment they began to dig up the earth. They had been granted permission to enter the property to view the monument and had exceeded such authority when they commenced their excavation. *Webb v Ireland* [1988] I.R. 353.

DPP v McMahon [1987]

Plainclothes members of the Gardaí entered the defendant's premises in order to investigate breaches of the Gaming and Lotteries Act 1956. The Gardaí did not have a search warrant as required under the Act when they entered the premises. The defendant argued that the evidence obtained as a result of the search was inadmissible. The Gardaí justified their entry inter alia on the basis that they had implied permission to enter the premises as ordinary members of the public.

Held: The Gardaí had abused their right of entry and were trespassers. The implied invitation bestowed on the public to enter licensed premises did not extend to members of the Gardaí whose sole purpose for entry was extraneous to the terms of the invitation. *DPP v McMahon* [1987] I.L.R.M. 87.

Key Principle: If a trespass is ongoing, it will be deemed to be a continuing trespass and will give rise to actions *de die in diem* (as long as it lasts).

Holmes v Wilson [1839]

The defendants trespassed on the plaintiff's land when installing buttresses to support the construction of a road.
Held: The defendant was held liable for a continuing trespass when, following an initial action for trespass, he then failed to remove the offending buttresses from the plaintiff's property. *Holmes v Wilson* (1839) 10 A. & E. 503.

Key Principle: Save where prescribed under statute, an action will lie where the trespass takes place above or below the land.

Kelsen v Imperial Tobacco Co [1957]

The plaintiff and defendant owned adjoining premises. The defendant erected an advertising sign on the outside of his building. The sign overhung the plaintiff's property by a number of inches.
Held: The defendant had committed a trespass as there was an encroachment into the plaintiff's airspace. *Kelsen v Imperial Tobacco Co* [1957] 2 Q.B. 334.

Bernstein v Skyviews Ltd [1978]

The plaintiff owned a country house and brought an action in trespass against the defendant who was in the business of taking aerial photographs of certain properties and had taken such photographs of the plaintiff's property.
Held: The plaintiff's action was unsuccessful. The court restricted the ownership of airspace by a landowner and held that where the intrusion occurred at a certain height so that it did not interfere with the plaintiff's use or enjoyment of the property it could not be actionable

as a trespass. Otherwise, as Griffiths J. opined, it could lead to the absurdity of a trespass being committed by "a satellite every time it passes over a suburban garden". *Bernstein v Skyviews Ltd* [1978] Q.B. 479.

Cox v Moulsey [1848]

The defendant drove a stake into the subsoil of property which was owned by the plaintiff.

Held: The defendant was liable in trespass to the plaintiff who was the owner of the subsoil. *Cox v Moulsey* (1848) 5 C.B. 533.

DEFENCES TO TRESPASS TO LAND

1. Consent

Consent provides a good defence to an action in trespass to land unless the entrant abuses that right of entry (*DPP v McMahon* [1987] I.L.R.M. 87). Where an entrant enters on foot of a contractual agreement, the right to enter can only be revoked according to the terms of the agreement (*Hurst v Picture Theatres Ltd* [1915] 1 K.B. 1).

2. Necessity

A person entering property without permission may have a defence to an action in trespass where it can be established that such entry was on foot of an emergency. However, it must be shown that the entry was reasonable in the circumstances (*Cope v Sharpe* [1912] 1 K.B. 496).

3. Lawful Authority

Where a person enters property with lawful justification, he or she will not be held liable under the tort of trespass to land, provided that he or she does not abuse his right of entry (*DPP v McMahon* [1987] I.L.R.M. 87).

15. NUISANCE

INTRODUCTION

The tort of nuisance protects the plaintiff's right to the use and enjoyment of his or her property from the unjustified or unreasonable interference by neighbouring owners or occupiers of property. Defendants have been found liable in nuisance for activities ranging from the creation of excessive noise (*Halsey v Esso Petroleum Co Ltd* [1961] 1 W.L.R. 683) to the discharge of offensive smells (*Rapier v London Tramways Co* [1893] 2 Ch. 588) and the running of brothels (*Thompson-Schwab v Costaki* [1956] 1 All E.R. 652).

Despite the development of negligence and the continued existence of claims such as trespass to land and *Rylands v Fletcher*, the tort of nuisance continues to remain an important cause of action in disputes involving property. Nuisance has distinct advantages over a claim for negligence, for example. First, the assessment of the defendant's conduct is more favourable to the plaintiff as the "reasonableness" of the defendant's behaviour is assessed from the point of view of its impact on the plaintiff after the nuisance has been created rather than from the point of view of assessing the defendant's behaviour before the nuisance has occurred. Secondly, the remedies for an action in nuisance are more varied than those available for an action in negligence e.g. an injunction may be available in an action for nuisance whereas damages are the sole remedy for a claim in negligence.

PUBLIC NUISANCE

Key Principle: A public nuisance is committed where the reasonable comfort of the plaintiff as a member of the public is unreasonably interfered with. Public nuisance is a crime. In a civil action for public nuisance it is the Attorney General that brings the action, thus the guilty party will not face a multitude of actions by members of the public arising from the same wrong (*Smith v Wilson* [1903] 2 I.R. 45).

Attorney-General v P.Y.A. Quarries Ltd [1957]

The defendant's quarrying activities caused significant disturbance to the local neighbourhood which consisted of a number of houses and adjoining highways. The defendant's actions created a certain amount of noise, dust and vibrations which caused a discomfort to the surrounding public. The defendant argued that the cause of action was one in private nuisance and not public nuisance.

Held: The defendant was liable for creating a public nuisance. The court held that a cause of action in public nuisance exists where the reasonable comfort of a certain class of the public is materially affected by the defendant's actions. The question as to what amounts to a "class" for the purposes of the action depends on the individual facts of the case. *Attorney-General v P.Y.A. Quarries Ltd* [1957] 2 Q.B. 169.

Wandsworth L.B.C. v Railtrack [2001]

A number of pigeons began roosting under a railway bridge which was under the control of the defendant. As a result, the droppings from the pigeons created a nuisance and a danger for members of the public passing below on the footpath.

Held: The defendant was liable in public nuisance for the danger and inconvenience created by the pigeon's droppings. While they did not own the pigeons, the defendant was responsible for the nuisance they created. *Wandsworth L.B.C. v Railtrack* [2001] E.W.C.A. Civ 1236.

Key Principle: A private individual may bring an action in public nuisance where he or she can establish that he or she has suffered particular or special damage, over and above that suffered by ordinary members of the general public.

Boyd v Great Northern Railway [1895]

The plaintiff was a doctor who was delayed for over twenty minutes due to the defendant's negligent failure to lift the gates at a level crossing.

Held: The plaintiff was entitled to recover damages for what was essentially a public nuisance. The doctor was able to establish that he had suffered particular damage which was not suffered by ordinary members of the public who were similarly delayed. The doctor's time had monetary value and the delay caused him appreciable damage which had not been suffered by other members of the public. *Boyd v Great Northern Railway* [1895] 2 I.R. 555.

Smith v Wilson [1903]

The plaintiff was an elderly farmer who regularly walked a certain route to the local market. The defendant obstructed the plaintiff's path and he was then required to take a much longer route to reach the market and on some occasions he had to pay for transport in order to reach his destination.

Held: The plaintiff was entitled to bring an action for damages in nuisance. The court was satisfied that the farmer had established that he had suffered particular damage in the form of inconvenience and financial expense. *Smith v Wilson* [1903] 2 I.R. 45 (KBD).

PRIVATE NUISANCE

Introduction

Private nuisance involves the unreasonable interference by the owner or occupier of property with a neighbour's use and enjoyment of their property. Such "unreasonable interference" may involve material damage to the plaintiff's property itself; interference with the plaintiff's enjoyment of that property, or an interference with servitudes.

MATERIAL DAMAGE TO PROPERTY

Key Principle: Where the nuisance causing material damage arises because of the defendant's failure to act in respect of a natural hazard on the property, then the defendant will be found liable for the damage caused where he or she knew or should have known of the risks posed by the hazard and did nothing to prevent those risks from materializing.

Leakey v National Trust [1980]

The defendant owned property adjoining the plaintiff's. Due to unusual weather conditions, topsoil placed on the defendant's property slid onto his neighbour's causing damage. There was also a very real danger that further damage could be caused if the defendant did not take remedial action. The plaintiff brought an action in nuisance and sought an injunction to remove the topsoil.

Held: The court found in favour of the defendant on the basis that the events were foreseeable and the defendant should have taken remedial action. *Leakey v National Trust* [1980] Q.B. 485 (CA).

Lynch v Hetherton [1990]

The plaintiff's car was damaged by a tree which fell from the defendant's property (which was adjoining the highway). Evidence was introduced into court to the effect that the tree had been rotten from the inside (but this was not obvious to the casual observer). The farmer had inspected the trees prior to the accident, but had not employed an expert to examine them.
Held: The defendant was not liable. In the words of O'Hanlon J: "... that a landowner having on his lands a tree or trees adjoining a highway or his neighbour's land is bound to take such care as a reasonable and prudent landowner would take to guard against the danger of damage being done by a falling tree." *Lynch v Hetherton* [1990] I.L.R.M. 857.

Key Principle: Where the nuisance causing material damage arises because of the defendant's positive conduct, the reasonableness of such conduct will be assessed from the point of view of the effect it had on the plaintiff's enjoyment of his or her property after the nuisance has occurred.

Patterson v Murphy [1978]

The plaintiffs purchased a property in a rural area. The defendant began carrying out quarrying operations on the property next to the plaintiffs'. Blasting operations commenced on a regular basis causing cracks to appear on the walls of the plaintiffs' house and the vibrations caused a window to break. The plaintiffs were unable to sit in their back garden from the dust which came from the neighbouring property.
Held: The defendant's activities gave rise to an actionable nuisance. The standard of comfort which the plaintiffs were entitled to enjoy was that which a normal person living in a rural agricultural area could expect to enjoy. *Patterson v Murphy* [1978] I.L.R.M. 85.

UNREASONABLE INTERFERENCE WITH THE USE AND ENJOYMENT OF PROPERTY

Introduction

Where a plaintiff brings an action in private nuisance because his or her use or enjoyment of property has been interfered with, he or she must establish that such interference is substantial and unreasonable. The reasonableness of the defendant's conduct is judged "according to the ordinary usages of mankind living in a particular society" (per Lord Wright in *Sedleigh-Denfield v O Callaghan* [1940] A.C. 880). Factors which may influence a finding of unreasonable interference may include the following:

1. LOCALITY

Key Principle: The environment in which the activity is taking place will be a factor in deciding whether that activity amounted to an unreasonable interference.

Sturges v Bridgman [1879]

A confectioner had for more than twenty years been using industrial pestles and mortars as part of his business. The plaintiff was a doctor who lived next door, who built an extension consulting room at the end of his back garden next door to the confectioner's business. The noise and vibrations created a nuisance which disturbed the plaintiff's patients. **Held:** The confectioner was liable for nuisance. The activity carried on by the confectioner had the effect of disturbing the plaintiff's neighbours and given the locality such disturbance was unreasonable. *Sturges v Bridgman* (1879) 11 Ch.D. 852.

O'Kane v Campbell [1985]

The defendant's shop was located on the corner of North Circular Road (a primarily commercial area) and Glengariff Parade (which was almost completely residential). The defendant commenced trading as a 24-hour shop, which caused disturbance to the plaintiff who lived on Glengariff Parade. The court noted that the noise was the inevitable result of persons using the shop throughout the night. It was noted by the court that if the shop had been located wholly on Glengariff Parade, it would have amounted to a clear and actionable nuisance on account of the traffic congestion and noise created. If the shop was wholly located on the North Circular Road, the court doubted whether any actionable nuisance would have existed. **Held:** In recognition of the opposing interests of the parties, the court granted an order restraining the defendants from trading between midnight and 6 am. *O'Kane v Campbell* [1985] I.R. 115.

Thompson-Schwab v Costaki [1956]

The claimant lived in 13 Chesterfield Street in London which was a good class residential street. The defendants were prostitutes who were located at 12 Chesterfield Street. The claimant argued that the defendants were creating a nuisance by operating a brothel from number 12 and because they were soliciting on the street directly outside.

Held: The activities of the defendants were such that they constituted, "a sensible interference with the comfortable and convenient enjoyment of his [the claimant's] residence." *Thompson-Schwab v Costaki* [1956] 1 All E.R. 652.

2. DURATION

Key Principle: The longer the interference continues, the more likely it will be found to be unreasonable. The interference need not be continuous but may be intermittent.

Harrison v Southwark and Vauxhall Water Co [1891]

The defendants carried out works adjoining the plaintiff's property. As a result a certain amount of noise and vibration was created which caused considerable disturbance to the plaintiff.

Held: The noise was only temporary and the work was necessary. As such, an action in nuisance was not successful. *Harrison v Southwark and Vauxhall Water Co* [1891] 2 Ch. 409.

Leeman v Montagu [1936]

A number of cockerels were crowing between 2 am and 7 am next to a residential area.

Held: The nature and duration of the noise amounted to a nuisance. *Leeman v Montagu* [1936] 2 All E.R. 1677.

Halpin v Tara Mines Ltd [1976–77]

The plaintiffs were living a rural area and brought an action in nuisance arising from the noise and vibrations which emanated from their neighbour's prospecting activities.

Held: The noises emanating from the defendant's activities were not of the type one would normally expect to find in such a locality.

Gannon J. noted that where such noises come at irregular times they can "be more disagreeable than noises which form part of the norm for the locality, such as passing traffic." *Halpin v Tara Mines Ltd* [1976–77] I.L.R.M. 28 (HC)

3. SENSITIVITY

Key Principle: If the damage is caused because the plaintiff, or his or her property, is considered to be "hyper-sensitive" the court may find that a nuisance has not occurred.

Robinson v Kilvert (1889)

The defendant raised the temperature in his cellar. The heat from the cellar damaged the plaintiff's stock of brown paper stored in the room above. He brought an action in nuisance as a result.
Held: The damage suffered by the plaintiff arose from the abnormal sensitivity of the paper and the defendant was found not liable as the defendant had not acted unreasonably. *Robinson v Kilvert* (1889) 41 Ch. 88.

4. PUBLIC UTILITY

Key Principle: The social utility of the defendant's actions may be taken into account when considering whether the activity is unreasonable. Greater latitude will be granted to an individual who undertakes an activity which is in the common good, notwithstanding that it may prove to be a nuisance to other members of the public.

Clifford v Drug Treatment Centre Board [1997]

An action in nuisance was brought against the defendant who operated a drug treatment centre near the plaintiff's home. The plaintiff applied for an injunction seeking to reduce the number of patients that were being treated by the defendants.
Held: The court refused to grant an injunction. The work being carried out by the defendant was in the public good. However, the court did prohibit the defendants from increasing beyond the existing levels the number of patients treated. *Clifford v Drug Treatment Centre Board* High Court, November 7, 1997.

Miller v Jackson [1977]

The plaintiff's back garden was located near a local cricket ground. A number of cricket balls were hit from the ground into the plaintiff's property. The plaintiff sued the defendant in negligence and nuisance. The defendant argued that it was in the interests of the common good that the sport of cricket be protected and that the granting of an injunction would not be in the public interest in the circumstances.

Held: The court found that the activity of the defendant could amount to a nuisance. However, the court, commenting on the importance of the sport of cricket to English society held that it would be contrary to public policy to grant an injunction. *Miller v Jackson* [1977] Q.B. 966.

Key Principle: The convenience of the public is not considered a relevant factor in determining whether the defendant's behavior was unreasonable.

Bellew v Cement Ltd [1948]

An action in nuisance was brought against the defendant as a result of noise and dust created by the defendant's cement factory. The defendant argued that this conduct did not amount to nuisance as the activity was in the public interest due to a shortage of cement following World War II, a shortage that was being alleviated by the acts alleged to constitute a nuisance against the plaintiff.

Held: Despite the shortage of cement in the country the court ordered that the factory desist from the offending behaviour. *Bellew v Cement Ltd* [1948] I.R. 61.

Key Principle: If it can be established that the plaintiff's property would have been damaged by the defendant's conduct (irrespective of its abnormal sensitivity) then an action in nuisance will be successful notwithstanding the plaintiff's sensitive nature.

McKinnon Industries v Walker [1951]

The plaintiff's orchids were damaged as a result of noxious fumes created by the defendant's factory. The defendant argued that an action in nuisance could not succeed due to the plaintiff's abnormal sensitivity.

Held: The plaintiff's action in nuisance was successful. It was established in court that the noxious fumes in question would have damaged the flowers regardless of whether they were of a sensitive nature or not. *McKinnon Industries v Walker* [1951] 3 D.L.R. 557.

5. MALICE

Key Principle: In determining whether the offending behaviour is unreasonable, the courts will take the motivation of the defendant in undertaking the activity into consideration.

Christie v Davie [1893]

The plaintiff was a music teacher who carried out music lessons in his home. His next door neighbour was annoyed by the sound of the plaintiff's students and in response he banged dustbins lids against the partition wall in order to disrupt the plaintiff's work.
Held: The defendant's actions, motivated as they were by malice, amounted to nuisance. *Christie v Davie* [1893] 1 Ch. 316.

Hollywood Silver Fox Farm Ltd v Emmett [1936]

The defendant ordered his son to fire guns on his own land as near as possible to the plaintiff's breeding pens in order that the latter's vixen might refuse to breed or miscarry.
Held: Although the defendant was entitled to shoot on his own land for pleasure or to control the rabbit population, the defendant in this case was motivated by malice and as such the defendant was found liable in nuisance. *Hollywood Silver Fox Farm Ltd v Emmett* [1936] 2 K.B. 468.

WHO CAN SUE?

Key Principle: Initially, only an individual with a legal interest in the property concerned could bring an action in negligence.

Malone v Laskey [1907]

The occupier's wife suffered injury when a bracket fell from a wall in the family home allegedly because of vibrations which came from next door. She brought an action in nuisance against the neighbours.

Held: The plaintiff was the wife of the occupier of the house and, as such, she was considered to be a licensee and was precluded from bringing an action in nuisance as she did not have any legal entitlement to the property. *Malone v Laskey* [1907] 2 K.B. 141.

Key Principle: More recently, the Irish judiciary has adopted a more lenient attitude in determining whether a plaintiff has locus standi to sue in private nuisance. It would now appear that a plaintiff will be deemed to have sufficient locus standi to bring an action where he or she is deemed to have been in occupation of the land.

Molumby v Kearns [1999]

The plaintiffs brought an action in nuisance regarding the operations of an industrial estate which was neighbouring their properties. The defendant argued inter alia that some of the plaintiffs had no locus standi to bring the action as they had not established that they had a sufficient legal interest in the properties.
Held: The court was satisfied that each of the plaintiffs was in occupation of the properties in question and that was sufficient to entitle them to bring the action. *Molumby v Kearns*, High Court, O'Sullivan J., January 19, 1999.

WHO MAY BE LIABLE?

1. The creator of the nuisance

Key Principle: The creator of the nuisance will be liable for the nuisance. The creator of the nuisance need not be in occupation of the property for these purposes.

Southport Corporation v Esso Petroleum [1956]

The defendant's oil tanker ran aground and the skipper of the ship decided to unload some of its cargo of oil into the sea in order to avoid the ship breaking up and causing loss of life. The oil caused a great deal of pollution and an action in nuisance was brought against the owners of the ship. The defendants pleaded that the actions of the skipper were motivated by necessity in order to protect the lives of his crew.

Held: The court found that a nuisance had been committed notwithstanding the fact that the defendants had not been in occupation of the land at the time. However, the defence of necessity which had been pleaded was accepted and the defendants avoided liability. *Southport Corporation v Esso Petroleum* [1956] A.C. 218.

2. The Landlord

Key Principle: A landlord will be liable where he or she authorises the creation or the maintenance of the nuisance. Such authorisation may be express or implied.

Goldfarb v Williams & Co [1945]

The defendant leased a building to a sports and athletic club. The lessees held dances and other social activities in the club, much to the annoyance of the plaintiffs and an action in nuisance followed.
Held: The lessees had been using the club in a reasonable manner under the terms of the lease. The defendant was aware from negotiations with the lessees that it was their intention to hold various social functions in the premises. The defendant was therefore found liable in nuisance for facilitating the nuisance. *Goldfarb v Williams & Co* [1945] I.R. 433 (HC).

Tetley v Chitty [1986]

A go-kart club was granted a lease over the defendant's property for racing purposes. This activity created a lot of noise and dust which disturbed the defendant's neighbours.
Held: The defendant as an occupier was liable for the club's activities. Granting permission to the club to use the land for these purposes amounted to an authorisation of the nuisance. *Tetley v Chitty* [1986] 1 All E.R. 663.

3. The Occupier

Key Principle: Where the occupier creates the nuisance or authorises it he or she will be liable for it. Further, an occupier will be liable where he or she fails to take reasonable steps to abate the nuisance once he or she becomes aware of it.

Vitalograph (Ireland) Ltd v Ennis UDC and Clare CC **[1997]**

A number of companies carrying out business in an industrial estate sought an injunction against the defendants after a number of Traveller families had parked on a piece of land owned by the defendant which was situated at the entrance of the industrial estate. The defendant argued that it was not liable as the Travellers had no authorisation to be present on the property.

Held: The defendant had failed to take steps (other than writing a letter) to remove the families from the premises. Their presence was undoubtedly a nuisance as they had brought with them a number of vehicles, some horses and large amounts of scrap metal. The defendant was found to have adopted the nuisance and an injunction was granted against the defendant ordering it to restrain the nuisance. *Vitalograph (Ireland) Ltd v Ennis UDC and Clare CC*, High Court, April 23, 1997.

DEFENCES TO NUISANCE

1. Legislative Authority

Key Principle: What might otherwise be considered as a nuisance will not be actionable where it is authorised under statute.

Kelly v Dublin CC **[1986]**

The defendant was carrying out road works construction. The plaintiff brought an action in nuisance. His home was adjoining a depot used by the defendant and the noise and fumes created by trucks entering and leaving the depot every working day caused considerable annoyance to the plaintiff. The defendant contended that it was authorised to create such nuisance by statutory authority.

Held: The defendant's activities in relation to the depot amounted to an actionable nuisance. The statutory authority to create a nuisance only applied to the maintenance and construction of roads and did not extend to activities ancillary to that purpose, i.e. the use of the depot. *Kelly v Dublin CC*, February 21, 1986, High Court.

2. Prescription

Key Principle: In private nuisance, 20 years continuance of the activity will legitimise it. The activity must have been continuing with the knowledge of the owner and without his or her objection. For prescription to apply, the activity must have continued for 20 years from the date it became a nuisance to the plaintiff.

Sturges v Bridgman [1879]

The plaintiff who was a doctor, lived in a residential area. He built a consulting room at the end of his back garden. The defendant who was his next door neighbour, had been using heavy machinery, without complaint, at the back of his own garden for over 20 years before the plaintiff had constructed his consulting room. The noise emanating from the defendant's property caused annoyance to the plaintiff and he brought an action in nuisance. The defendant pleaded the defence of prescription.

Held: The plaintiff was successful in his action. The defendant's activities only became a nuisance once it affected the plaintiff in the reasonable enjoyment of his property. It was irrelevant that the defendant had been pursuing the activity for years prior to that point. Time ran from the date the consulting room was built and the noise became a nuisance to the plaintiff. *Sturges v Bridgman* (1879) 11 Ch.D. 852.

Commentary

It should be noted that it is an ineffectual defence for the defendant to plead that the plaintiff came to the nuisance. Thus, in *Sturges* (above) it was not open to the defendant to plead that he had been carrying out the activity for a number of years prior to the plaintiff's arrival. Similarly, in *Bliss v Hall* (1838) 4 Bing NC 183 it was found that emissions (which had been in existence for three years before the plaintiff arrived) were held to amount to a nuisance as the plaintiff had come to the house with all rights which the common law affords, and one of them is a right to wholesome air.

3. Consent

Key Principle: Where the plaintiff consents to the activity in question, an action in nuisance cannot be brought.

Thomas v Lewis [1878]

The defendant opened a quarry and granted grazing rights to the plaintiff. The plaintiff then brought an action in nuisance alleging that the plaintiff's quarrying was interfering with his reasonable enjoyment of the land.

Held: The plaintiff had impliedly consented to the impugned acts and this constituted a defence to an action based on the tort of nuisance. *Thomas v Lewis* (1878) 4 Ex. D. 18.

16. THE RULE IN *RYLANDS V FLETCHER*

INTRODUCTION

Recovery of damages under Irish tort law is generally based on the principle that the plaintiff must establish that the defendant was at fault for the damage caused. However, there are a number of exceptions to this general rule whereby liability will be imposed on the defendant irrespective of fault. One such exception is the rule in *Rylands v Fletcher*. This is a land-based tort that was developed alongside the tort of nuisance and prior to the establishment of the modern principles of negligence following *Donoghue v Stevenson* in 1932 and must be viewed in light of these origins. Indeed, its survival to this day, some would argue, is simply the result of historical accident.

THE PRINCIPLE

Key Principle: Any person who brings or keeps on his or her land, anything liable to cause mischief if it escapes, will be prima facie liable for all the damage which is a natural consequence of any such escape.

Rylands v Fletcher [1868]

The defendant engaged independent contractors to construct a reservoir for a mill. During the construction, a number of old mine shafts were discovered, but it was not realised that these indirectly connected with the plaintiff's neighbouring mine. The contractors were negligent in not ensuring that the filled in shafts could bear the weight of the water and some time later, the partially filled reservoir burst through and flooded the plaintiff's mine. The defendant had not been negligent as he had engaged an apparently competent independent contractor to construct the reservoir. An action in trespass to land could not be brought as the damage was not caused as a direct consequence of the defendant's actions and an action in nuisance at that time could not be sustained as there had only been one escape onto the defendant's property.

Held: The House of Lords imposed liability on the defendant establishing a rule which stated that he was strictly liable for the damage caused by the escape of a dangerous thing stored on his land. This became known as the rule in *Rylands v Fletcher* [1868] L.R. 3 H.L. 330.

Commentary

While the House of Lords approved the earlier decision in this case reached by Blackburn J. in the Court of Exchequer Chamber, the judgment of Lord Cairns did create some confusion as to the precise scope of the rule. While Blackburn J.'s ruling focused on the phrase *likely to do mischief if it escapes* which appears to involve some element of foreseeability, Lord Cairns justified the imposition of liability based on what he termed the plaintiff's *non-natural* use of the land. Thus, it would now seem that a critical element of the action is that the plaintiff establishes that the use to which the land was put was non-natural.

ELEMENTS OF THE CAUSE OF ACTION

"*Non-natural use*"

Key Principle: A defendant will be considered to have used his or her property in a non-natural manner where he or she uses the property in an unusual or extraordinary way. The use must be extraordinary and must bring with it an increased danger to others and is not for the general benefit of the community.

Rickards v Lothian [1913]

The plaintiff was leasing a second floor premises as offices. Upon arrival to the premises one morning, he found that the offices had been flooded due to a washbasin which had overflowed in the defendant's upstairs bathroom. The basin had been blocked by a malicious third party.
Held: The defendant was not liable. In order to amount to a non-natural use it must be established that the land was used for a purpose which was extraordinary and brought with it an increased danger to others. The storage of water for domestic purposes was necessary for the general benefit of the community and the manner in which the flooding occurred did not amount to a non-natural use in these circumstances. *Rickards v Lothian* [1913] A.C. 263.

Mason v Levy Auto Parts of England Ltd [1967]

The defendants stored crates of combustible material on their land. The material was mysteriously set on fire. This fire damaged the plaintiff's property.

Held: Given the character of the surrounding neighbourhood and the type of material which was being stored by the defendants, the court found that the defendants' activities amounted to a non-natural use of his land and he was liable under the rule in *Rylands v Fletcher*. *Mason v Levy Auto Parts of England Ltd* [1967] 2 Q.B. 530.

Transco v Stockport Metropolitan Borough Council [2004]

The defendant owned a block of flats. These flats were supplied with water through high pressure pipes which supplied tanks in the basement of the flats. One of these pipes was damaged and began leaking. It was some time before the leak was discovered and repaired. The water which escaped ran into an old landfill before running along an old railway line. The plaintiff had laid a gas pipe which was supported by an embankment next to the railway line. The water from the leaked pipe washed away the embankment beneath the gas pipe which left it without adequate support. The claimant argued that the defendant was liable for the cost of repairing the supporting structure for the gas pipe.

Held: The defendant was not liable under the rule in *Rylands v Fletcher*. In particular, the House of Lords held that the water pipe leading to the block of flats could not be considered a non-natural use of the property. While the pipe might have been larger than domestic water pipes it could not be said that it was so much larger that it represented an extraordinary danger. *Transco v Stockport Metropolitan Borough Council* [2004] 2 A.C. 1.

Commentary

The precise definition of "non-natural use" has plagued the tort. A literal interpretation of the words would indicate that any use of the property which does not accord with nature could be considered non-natural. Yet, it would appear from *Rylands* that it is only commercial activities where such activity brings with it an increased danger to the community with no discernible benefit which fall within the definition. Thus, in *Rylands* the storage of water artificially for commercial purposes (the reservoir) was deemed to be an unnatural use whereas water stored for domestic purposes in *Rickards* was deemed to be a "natural" use. This confusion in terminology just adds to the uncertainty surrounding the tort and its application.

"Escape"

Key Principle: The thing must escape from the plaintiff's property to a place which is outside his or her control.

Read v Lyons **[1947]**

The plaintiff was employed as an inspector of munitions. She was injured when a shell exploded while she was inspecting the defendant's premises. Negligence was not alleged on the part of the defendant and a claim was made under *Rylands*.
Held: The House of Lords rejected the claim. The rule in *Rylands v Fletcher* requires that there must be an escape from the defendant's premises to a place which is outside his or her control. This did not occur here as the plaintiff was injured by the explosion while inside the defendant's premises. *Read v Lyons* [1947] A.C. 156.

Commentary

This decision has been criticised on the basis that there is something inherently unfair in a rule that did not find for the plaintiff in circumstances where she was injured prior to leaving the defendant's premises, but would have entitled her to succeed had she been injured by the blast as she was about to enter the premises, having met the "escape" requirement of the rule. Indeed, Lord Porter in the House of Lords accepted this criticism as being valid, but was of the opinion that as the rule in *Rylands v Fletcher* was an exception to the principle of fault liability, it must be narrowly interpreted. The requirement of escape was justified on the basis that the rule imposes strict liability and whereas this can be considered fair in the event of an escape from one property to another outside the defendant's control, someone entering onto the defendant's property can only expect that the defendant will take reasonable care for their safety.

"Damage"

Key Principle: While the escape need not be foreseeable, liability under *Rylands* may not now exist for unforeseeable damage caused by the escape.

Cambridge Water Co Ltd v Eastern Counties Leather Plc **[1994]**

The defendant was a leather manufacturer who used the chemical solvent PCE in its tanning process. Continual small spillages had gradually built up a pool of liquid under the land and contaminated the aquifer from which the plaintiffs drew their supply of water. As a result it cost the plaintiffs nearly £1 million to find an alternative source of water. At the time of the contamination, it would not have been foreseeable to the skilled person that the chemical would accumulate in the aquifer, nor, even if this could have been foreseen, was it foreseeable that there would be any significant danger to the plaintiff's water supply.

Held: The plaintiff's action in *Rylands v Fletcher* failed. The House of Lords held that in order to succeed under the rule, it must be established that the type of harm suffered as a result of the escape was reasonably foreseeable. While some damage may have been foreseeable as a result of the spillage, the damage that actually occurred was wholly unforeseeable. *Cambridge Water Co Ltd v Eastern Counties Leather Plc* [1994] 2 A.C. 264.

Commentary

The requirement introduced by the *Cambridge* decision that the type of damage must be reasonably foreseeable has brought the rule in *Rylands v Fletcher* closer to the tort of negligence. This move has introduced the element of fault into the application of what is otherwise a strict liability tort. Indeed, the High Court of Australia in *Burnie Port Authority v General Jones Pty Ltd* (1994) 179 C.L.R. 520, has effectively abolished the rule, stating that the laws of negligence can adequately deal with the situations governed by the rule. In *Burnie,* the court found that a non-delegable duty of care for hazardous activities rested on the shoulders of the defendant in such circumstances. McMahon & Binchy in their leading textbook *Law of Torts*, 3rd edn, (Butterworths, 2000), p.734 have commented that a strong argument exists for adopting the *Burnie* approach, particularly when one has regard for the devastating critique of the rule undertaken by the Australian High Court in that case.

DEFENCES

1. Act of a Stranger

Key Principle: A defendant will not be liable for an escape caused by the unanticipated independent act of a stranger.

Rickards v Lothian [1913]

The plaintiff was leasing a second floor premises as offices. Upon arrival to the premises one morning, he found that the offices had been flooded due to a washbasin which had overflowed in the defendant's upstairs bathroom. The basin had been blocked by a malicious third party.
Held: The defendant was not liable. The court found that the malicious actions of a third party which could not have been foreseen by the plaintiff provided a good defence. *Rickards v Lothian* [1913] A.C. 263.

Perry v Kendrick Transport Ltd [1956]

The defendant had parked a disused bus on his property. The petrol had been drained from the bus, but an unknown third party had removed the fuel cap from the tank. Two young boys lit a match and threw it into the empty fuel tank causing an explosion. Another child, the plaintiff, was badly burned as a result.
Held: The defendant was not liable. The defendant could not have foreseen nor anticipated the actions of other parties which led to the explosion. *Perry v Kendrick Transport Ltd* [1956] 1 All E.R. 557.

2. Act of God

Key Principle: A defendant may be excused liability under the rule in *Rylands v Fletcher* if the harm was caused by an act of God.

Superquinn Ltd v Bray UDC [1998]

The plaintiff claimed damages for loss caused by flooding in the wake of Hurricane Charlie. The fourth-named defendant, Coillte Teoranta, was joined in the proceedings on the basis that it had created an artificial dam on the river that had contributed to the flood that damaged the plaintiff's property. The fourth-named defendant argued that it was not liable as the storm that created the flood was an act of God.

Held: The defence succeeded. Laffoy J. commented that the proper test was whether the storm in question could reasonably have been anticipated or guarded against by the defendant. *Superquinn Ltd v Bray UDC*, unreported, High Court, February 18, 1998.

3. Consent

Key Principle: Where the plaintiff has consented to the storage of the thing, no action can later be brought for any damage caused by its subsequent escape.

Kiddle v City Business Premises Ltd [1942]

The plaintiff leased a shop from the defendant which was one unit in a bigger building. The roof from the defendant's premises sloped towards the plaintiff's premises and when the defendant's drainage system was blocked as a result of wartime bombing, the plaintiff's premises were flooded.

Held: The defendant had not acted negligently in any way regarding the drainage system. An action in *Rylands v Fletcher* was unsuccessful as the court found that the plaintiff had impliedly consented to the drainage system when leasing the premises. *Kiddle v City Business Premises Ltd* [1942] 2 All E.R. 216.

4. Default of the Plaintiff

Key Principle: If the plaintiff's own actions caused the thing to escape, the rule will not apply.

Dunn v Birmingham Canal [1872]

The plaintiff was working in his mine which was placed under the defendant's canal. The plaintiff was fully aware of where the mine was positioned. As a result of his activities the mine was flooded by the canal above.

Held: The plaintiff's action was rejected. He was aware of the danger and had caused the escape himself. *Dunn v Birmingham Canal* [1872] LR 7 Q.B. 244.

17. PASSING OFF

The tort of passing off provides supplemental protection to a plaintiff in the goodwill of their business. The tort is designed to prevent another trader unlawfully passing off products and other services as those of the plaintiffs and is usually brought at the injunctive stage of an action. Essentially, the tort aims to ensure that traders do not use the same name, packaging and advertising as another trader in order that they may take advantage of that trader's good reputation by deceiving the buying public.

DEFINITION

The modern definition of passing off was provided in the English House of Lords decision in *Warnink v Town-end & Sons* [1979] 2 All E.R. 927. In that case, Lord Diplock identified the following as being the key elements in an action for passing off:

(1) a misrepresentation
(2) made by a trader in the course of a trade
(3) to prospective customers of his or ultimate customers or ultimate consumers of goods or services supplied by him
(4) which is calculated to injure the business or goodwill of another trader (in the sense that this is a reasonably foreseeable consequence); and
(5) which causes actual damage to a business or goodwill of the trader by whom the action is brought or will probably do so.

Goodwill/Reputation

Key Principle: In order to succeed in an action for passing off, the plaintiff must prove that he or she has established goodwill/reputation in the product or business.

Box Television Ltd v Haymarket Magazines Ltd [1997]

The plaintiff brought an action in passing off over the use of the word "the box" to describe televisions.

Held: The plaintiff's claim failed as he was unable to show a specific connection between the use of the phrase and his business i.e. that the use of the words "the box" was so synonymous with his business that by using the same phrase the defendant was causing confusion amongst the public regarding the two businesses. *Box Television Ltd v Haymarket Magazines Ltd* [1997] *The Times*, March 3, 1997.

Key Principle: The plaintiff must prove that they have established goodwill in the product or business. Goodwill has been defined as that which exists through a course of trading within a particular jurisdiction.

Anheuser-Busch Inc v Budejovicky Budvar Narodoni Podnik *(The Budweiser Case)* **[1984]**

Budweiser had been produced by the plaintiff as a brand name in the U.S. since the 19th century. The defendant produced the same beer under a similar name in Czechoslovakia and mainland Europe. Both parties agreed that the plaintiff could use the name in the US while the defendant could use the name in Europe. The defendant imported their product into the UK. The plaintiff attempted to prevent this by claiming that they had built up goodwill in the UK even though they had never sold their product in the country. The plaintiff argued that they had established such goodwill on the basis that consumers in the UK were familiar with their product through tourism, advertisements, American movies and so forth.

Held: The court rejected this argument. The plaintiff had nothing but a minimal trading existence within the country. Thus, the plaintiff had no goodwill in their product within that jurisdiction. Their lack of a trading existence in that jurisdiction meant that sales of their product could not be affected by the defendant's activities. *Anheuser-Busch Inc v Budejovicky Budvar Narodoni Podnik (The Budweiser Case)* [1984] F.S.R. 413.

Commentary

This narrow view of goodwill is not without its critics. It has been argued that this definition bears no relation to the realities of the modern marketplace. In the global marketplace knowledge of a product can cross international borders causing to it to have a reputation in jurisdictions where the trader has never traded. Healy highlights further criticisms of this view of goodwill. The first of these is the *loss of control* argument which provides that such an approach dilutes the exclusivity that the plaintiff enjoys in his or her product and allows cheap (and perhaps inferior) imitations to enter the market. The second is the *loss of expansion* argument which provides that such an approach to goodwill means that the plaintiff will lose the opportunity of expanding into new markets as they will already be flooded by the defendant's cheap imitations. In light of these criticisms, a wider approach towards the definition of goodwill has been adopted (Healy, *Principles of Irish Torts*, (Clarus Press, 2006) at 396).

Key Principle: An action in passing off will not only protect the goodwill which the plaintiff has built up in the business it may also extend to protecting the reputation of that business. Reputation is a broader concept than goodwill and a business may have reputation in a jurisdiction even though it has not traded there.

C & A Modes v C & A Modes Waterford **[1976]**

The plaintiff owned a department store which traded throughout the UK. The defendant opened a department store in the Republic of Ireland and called it C & A Modes (Waterford) Ltd. The plaintiff brought an action in passing off arguing that although it was not trading within the jurisdiction it had built up a reputation in the eyes of customers in the Republic through advertising on UK television and UK newspapers widely available in the Republic and also through cross-border shopping.
Held: In deciding what interest was to be protected the court adopted a wider view with Henchy J. stating that the guiding criteria is whether the name of the plaintiff's business "is known to the public in the area in which the defendant seeks to carry on his business . . . Goodwill does not stop at a frontier." The action for passing off was successful. *C & A Modes v C & A Modes Waterford* [1976] I.R. 198.

Confusion/Misrepresentation

Key Principle: It must be established that the public were confused between the competing businesses as a result of the defendant's actions i.e. they mistakenly believe that the businesses are the same or are associated each other. The test is whether the "careless and casual" person would have been confused.

Taittinger v Allbev Ltd [1993]

The defendant manufactured a non-alcoholic drink called Elderflower Champagne. This drink was sold in thick bottles with mushroomed-shaped corks and sold at £2.45 per bottle. The plaintiff argued that there was a risk that some members of the public would believe that this inferior product was in some way connected with Champagne or the Champagne region.

Held: There existed sufficient confusion amongst members of the public which justified the court's intervention. While many educated members of the public would conclude that there was no connection between the two products—particularly given the price—there was a danger that a significant portion of the public would associate the product with the defendant. *Taittinger SA v Allbev Ltd* [1993] F.S.R. 641.

Key Principle: A similarity in names between the competing businesses can give rise to a cause of action.

C & A Modes v C & A (Waterford) Ltd [1976]

The defendant opened a department store in the Republic of Ireland and used a name very similar to that used by the plaintiff for its department store which traded within the United Kingdom. The plaintiff sought to restrain the defendant from using the name on the basis that the defendant was seeking to exploit the Irish public's familiarity with C & A Modes whose reputation had been established in the Republic through advertising in British newspapers and through cross-border shopping.

Held: The plaintiff's action was successful. Given the nature of both businesses and the fact that the names were so similar it was likely that the public would be confused between the two businesses. *C & A Modes v C & A (Waterford) Ltd* [1976] I.R. 198.

Smithkline Beecham Plc v Antigen Pharmaceuticals Ltd [1999]

The plaintiff produced a painkiller called "Solpadeine" and brought an action in passing off against the defendant who produced a painkiller called "Solfen". The plaintiff argued that given the similarity in names between the products the public were likely to be confused.

Held: While the names were confusingly similar, the court stated that the argument was weakened by the fact that the drugs were only available over the counter. Thus, the chances of confusion were less likely because a qualified pharmacist would be aware of the distinction between the products. *Smithkline Beecham Plc v Antigen Pharmaceuticals Ltd* [1999] 2 I.L.R.M. 190 (HC)

Key Principle: A person may use his or her own name when marketing their product. However, he or she must only do so in a manner that does not mislead the public.

Jameson v Irish Distillers Co [1900]

The plaintiff produced the internationally famous whisky under the name of "John Jameson & Son." The defendant acquired a whisky producer entitled "William Jameson & Co." The defendant renamed the product as "Jameson's Whisky."
Held: Given the world-renowned reputation of the plaintiff's product, the defendant could not use the name in a similar manner unless some qualifying words were used to distinguish the products. *Jameson v Irish Distillers Co* [1900] 1 I.R. 43 (Ch.).

Key Principle: A similarity in the packaging of the products may give rise to a cause of action in passing off.

Polycell Products Ltd v O'Carroll [1959]

The plaintiff produced adhesive and sold it in a distinctive packaging. The plaintiff's product was called "Polycell". The defendant produced a product called "Clingcell" and sold it in a similar packaging to the plaintiff.
Held: The defendant was guilty of passing off. The court said that in determining whether the defendant was passing off its product as that of the plaintiff, regard must be had to the general "get up" of the packages. This would include: their size and shape, the material used, the colours, lettering, spacing of words and so forth. In other words, the court would consider the overall impression that the packaging would have made on the public. *Polycell Products Ltd v O'Carroll* [1959] Ir. Jur. Rep. 34.

Reckitt & Colman Products Ltd v Borden Inc [1990]

The plaintiff marketed its product "jif" lemon juice in a lemon-shaped container. A number of years later, the defendant (an American company) attempted to sell lemon juice in similar containers. The plaintiff sought an action restraining the defendant from selling their product in similar shaped containers.

Held: The defendant was guilty of passing off. Even though the defendant's product was named and labeled differently it was still found to have infringed the plaintiff's rights. The plaintiff had built up such goodwill in the product that when the public saw the containers they immediately associated them with the plaintiff. Had the defendant gone to greater lengths to distinguish its product from that of the plaintiff (through different colour lettering, for example) then it was unlikely that the plaintiff's action would have been successful. *Reckitt & Colman Products Ltd v Borden Inc.* [1990] 1 All E.R. 873.

Key Principle: Similarity of design will not give rise to a cause of action in passing off where sufficient efforts have been made to distinguish the competing products.

Adidas Sportsschuhfabricken KA v Charles O'Neill & Co Ltd. (the Adidas case) [1983]

The plaintiff (Adidas) brought an action against the defendant (O'Neills) an Irish company. The plaintiff alleged that the defendant was guilty of passing off when it produced sportswear clothing which bore stripes down the sides of the clothing in a fashion that was very similar to the plaintiff's internationally renowned three-stripe logo.

Held: There was no passing off. The defendant was well-established as a sportswear company in Ireland in its own right, particularly through its association with the Gaelic Athletic Association ("GAA"). Furthermore, the court held that the defendant, while copying a style, had sufficiently distinguished its product from that of the plaintiff i.e. through the printing of the name "O'Neills" on all their clothing. *Adidas Sportsschuhfabricken KA v Charles O'Neill & Co Ltd (the Adidas case)* [1983] I.L.R.M. 112 (SC).

R Griggs Group Ltd v Dunnes Stores [1996]

The plaintiff produced the world famous "Doc Marten" boots. It sought an injunction against the defendant who produced an inferior replica product. The plaintiff's boots were made of black leather with yellow stitching and a tab at the top of the heel. The defendant's product had a similar stitching and was of a similar style however the tab at the top of the heel had the words "*St. Bernard*" attached to it. The defendant argued that it was simply following a fashion trend and had done enough to distinguish its product from those of the plaintiff. **Held:** The court, while recognizing that the plaintiff had an arguable case, ultimately decided against granting an injunction on the basis that any possible damage (drop in worldwide sales of the plaintiff's boots) would be minimal and furthermore, any injunction granted at this stage would have had caused significant damage to the defendant. *R Griggs Group Ltd v Dunnes Stores*, High Court, October 4, 1996.

Key Principle: Similarity in advertising between the products may give rise to an action in passing off. However, the plaintiff must show that the public associates its product with the advertisement.

Cadbury Schweppes Ltd v Pub Squash Co [1981]

A lemon drink called "Solo" was packaged in a beer can and was advertised with a canoeist fighting the rapids. The defendant subsequently launched "Pub Squash", packaged in a beer can and with a similar advertisement.
Held: While the advertisement could lead to an action in passing off, in this case there was no evidence that the public had been deceived because the defendant's product was clearly distinguished from that of the plaintiff's. The injunction was refused. *Cadbury Schweppes Ltd v Pub Squash Co* [1981] 1 All E.R. 213 (HL).

Key Principle: It is the overall impression that the entire "get-up" leaves on reasonable members of the public which will determine whether there is confusion/misrepresentation.

Allergan Inc. v Ocean Healthcare Ltd [2008]

The plaintiff produced the famous pharmaceutical product "BOTOX" which contained a purified form of Botulinum Toxin Type A. BOTOX is a prescription only product which has therapeutic and cosmetic applications. It must be prescribed by a registered medical practitioner and can only be provided from a pharmacy and is administered by syringe. The defendant produced an anti-wrinkle cream called "BOTOINA". The plaintiff alleged that the name of the defendant's product and the way it was marketed was designed to cause confusion amongst the consuming public.

Held: In finding for the plaintiff, the court examined the question of "confusion" under the following headings:

(a) Visual Similarity—similarity in name. First four letters of each were similar.
(b) Aural Similarity—there was a phonetic similarity in the first part of each word.
(c) Conceptual Similarity—as both words were invented, the court found that they were not capable of conceptual similarity.
(d) Identity and/or Similarity of goods—there were many similarities in the way the products were presented. BOTOX is contained in a powder form in a glass vial which is then diluted with solution, before being drawn off with a syringe and injected. BOTOINA is a serum or cream in a vial which is drawn off into a syringe-like applicator and applied to the wrinkles or lines on the face. Both products are used for the reduction or amelioration of wrinkles or lines on the face.

Allergan Inc v Ocean Healthcare Ltd [2008] I.E.H.C. 189.

Key Principle: If there is a common course of trade or a common field of activity between the parties, then it will be more likely that confusion will occur amongst the public and will be less likely the plaintiff will suffer damage through loss of customers.

Harrods v Harrodian School Ltd [1996]

The famous department store (Harrods) brought an action against a boys' prep school that named itself the "Harrodian School". The plaintiff argued that the store's name had become so popular and synonymous with quality and class that it had created its own adjective "harrodian."

Held: Because the parties were in completely different fields of activity (department store vs boys' school) the court stated that it was unlikely that the public would be confused between the businesses and that it was even less likely that the plaintiff would suffer damage to its business. *Harrods v Harrodian School Ltd* [1996] R.P.C. 697.

Key Principle: The requirement of the "common field of activity" has proven to be an obstacle to celebrities and other well known personalities who wish to utilize the passing off action as a means of protecting their image rights.

McCulloch v Lewis A May (Produce Distributors) Ltd **[1947]**

The plaintiff was a well-known broadcaster of children's programmes for the BBC. He worked under the stage name of "Uncle Mac". As Uncle Mac, the plaintiff carried out other activities apart from broadcasting such as appearing at charity events and writing children's books. The defendant produced puffed wheat under the name of "Uncle Mac's Puffed Wheat" and marketed the product with slogans such as "Uncle Mac loves children – and children love Uncle Mac." The plaintiff sought an injunction and claimed damages as a result of this unauthorised use of his image which portrayed a false association between him and the defendant.
Held: Because there was no "common field of activity" between the defendant, a producer of breakfast cereals, and the plaintiff, a broadcaster, the court held that the chance of confusion amongst the public was eliminated and as a consequence no action in passing off could succeed. *McCulloch v Lewis A May (Produce Distributors) Ltd* [1947] 2 All E.R. 845.

Key Principle: The requirement of the "common course of activity" as a pre-requisite to an action in passing off may no longer be considered an essential requirement.

Irvine v Talksport Ltd **[2002]**

The plaintiff was Eddie Irvine, a famous Formula One racing driver. The defendant, in promoting their sports' radio station, had purchased a photograph of the plaintiff (who was then at the height of his fame as a racing car driver) from a sporting photograph agency. The original photograph showed the plaintiff holding a mobile phone to his ear. The defendant doctored the photograph so, instead of holding a phone, it appeared that the plaintiff was holding a portable radio which displayed the name of the defendant's radio station. The plaintiff brought an action in passing off regarding the distribution of the brochure featuring the doctored image. It was the plaintiff's contention that the defendant's image of him falsely implied that he had endorsed their product.

Held: Laddie J., recognising the realities of the modern marketplace and the importance of celebrity endorsement within it, held that the case was one to which passing off would apply. In his view, the modern law of passing off not only protected goodwill from unauthorised association with inferior products but also acknowledged that passing off would not allow the defendant to dilute or diminish the exclusivity that the plaintiff is entitled to in his own image. *Irvine v Talksport Ltd* [2002] E.W.H.C. 367.

Commentary

In Ireland, the enactment of the Privacy Bill 2006 could bring change to this area. Section 2(1) of the Bill provides that "a person who, wilfully and without lawful authority, violates the privacy of an individual commits a tort." Section 3(1) the Bill further provides that "the privacy which an individual is entitled is that which is reasonable in all the circumstances having regard to the rights of others and to the requirements of public order, public morality and the common good." The Bill provides examples of the type of behaviour—subject to s.3(1) and ss.5 and 6 of the Bill—which will amount to a breach of an individual's privacy including the following:

> "(c) to use the name, likeness or voice of the individual, without
>   the consent of that individual, for the purpose of—
>   (i) advertising or promoting the sale of, or trade in, any
>   property or service, or
>   (ii) financial gain to the said person,
>   if, in the course of such use, the individual concerned is
>   identified or, as a result of such use, is capable of being
>   identified, and the said person knew that that individual had
>   not given such consent ..."

Damage

Key Principle: The defendant must show that the misrepresentation of his or her goodwill/reputation caused damaged to his or her business.

Falcon Travel Ltd v Owners Abroad Group Plc [1991]

The plaintiff was a travel agency operating in Dublin and Wicklow. The defendant worked as a tour operator in the UK and was called the

Falcon Leisure Group. The UK company began to trade in Dublin as Falcon Leisure. The plaintiff received calls from the defendant and vice versa. The plaintiff sought an injunction. The defendant argued that there was no likelihood of the public confusing the companies. One was a tour operator and the other was a travel agent. There was no evidence that the plaintiff suffered actual damage to trade. There was evidence however, that the names of both companies had become submerged into one another in the minds of the public.

Held: As the passing off was unintentional and there was no actual damage, an injunction was not granted. However, the court did award damages in lieu of an injunction in order to pay for advertising which would educate the public as to the difference between the companies. *Falcon Travel Ltd v Owners Abroad Group Plc* [1991] 1 I.R. 175 (HC).

18. DAMAGES

INTRODUCTION

Damages are the primary remedy available to the plaintiff in an action for tort. Damages are awarded as financial compensation to the plaintiff because his or her legal rights have been infringed in some way. The main objective of awarding damages is to compensate the plaintiff (in monetary terms) for the wrong that has been done to him or her i.e. to put the plaintiff back into the position he or she was in before the incident occurred. Under Irish law, damages must be recovered once and for all. A plaintiff cannot later bring another action claiming more damages for the same wrong simply because the injury he or she suffered was greater than he or she realized. There are, of course, certain exceptions to this general rule e.g. continuing trespass.

CATEGORIES OF DAMAGES

1. Compensatory Damages

The main objective of this category of damages is to compensate the plaintiff for the harm that he or she has suffered. These damages may be subdivided into (a) Special Compensatory Damages and (b) General Compensatory Damages.

(a) Special Damages

Key Principle: Special damages are generally awarded for pecuniary loss and include damages for loss of earnings and medical expenses.

Reddy v Bates [1983]

The plaintiff suffered severe injuries in a car accident. The defendant appealed the quantum of the damages awarded.
Held: The award of special compensatory damages was reduced. It was noted that when making such an award in relation to the loss of future earnings the fact that the plaintiff's period of employment would be interrupted due to future unemployment, sickness etc. should be taken into consideration when assessing the quantum to be awarded under this

heading. The damages should have been discounted accordingly. *Reddy v Bates* [1983] I.R. 141 (SC).

Crilly v T & J Farrington [2000]

In accordance with s.2(1) of the Health (Amendment) Act 1986, the victims of a road traffic accident who have received or are entitled to receive damages for their injuries, will be charged directly by the hospital board for the costs of their medical care. In this case, the hospital and insurance company disagreed over the appropriate calculation of such charges. The Health Board argued that the true cost of a hospital stay should be calculated by the averaged daily cost of bed and board in the specific hospital. In this case the charge was £525 a day for a stay in Beaumont. On the other hand, the insurance company argued that the "charge" should be calculated under s.55 of the Health Act 1970 as a "maintenance charge" which worked out at £158 per night.

Held: Denham J. in the Supreme Court preferred the former of the two approaches. She noted that as the relevant section did not provide for a method as to how this charge was to be calculated, the charge would be upheld as long as the method of its calculation was reasonable. The approach suggested by the hospital was a reasonable one as it was "consistent and methodical." *Crilly v T & J Farrington* [2000] 1 I.L.R.M. 548 (HC).

(b) General Damages

Key Principle: General damages are awarded for non-pecuniary loss. These damages may include compensation for pain and suffering and loss of expectation of life.

Reddy v Bates [1983]

The plaintiff suffered severe injuries in a car accident. The defendant appealed the quantum of the award to the Supreme Court.

Held: Such damages were described as compensation in financial terms for the damage, both past and future for the pain suffering incurred by the plaintiff. *Reddy v Bates* [1983] I.R. 141 (SC).

Key Principle: An award of general damages for pain and suffering will take into consideration the plaintiff's own awareness of his or her pain and suffering.

Cooke v Walsh [1984]

The plaintiff suffered injuries which left him with a mental age of approximately one year.
Held: An award of £125,000 for general damages was considered excessive when one considered the fact that the plaintiff lacked an awareness of his plight. The award was reduced accordingly. *Cooke v Walsh* [1984] I.L.R.M. 208.

2. Aggravated Damages

Key Principle: Such damages are awarded in circumstances where the conduct of the defendant has aggravated the wrong done to the plaintiff. Such damages are justified on the basis that the defendant's outrageous conduct has further aggravated the injury to the plaintiff.

Connellan v St Joseph's Kilkenny [2006]

As a child, the plaintiff was subjected to sexual, racial and physical abuse at the hands of workers at a residential school.
Held: The general damages of £250,000 which were awarded were increased by an additional award of £50,000 in aggravated damages because of the outrageous conduct of the workers. *Connellan v St Joseph's Kilkenny*, High Court, March 21, 2006.

3. Nominal Damages

Key Principle: These damages are awarded in cases where the claim may be described as minor. These types of damages are awarded generally in torts that are actionable per se and the plaintiff has not suffered actual damage as a result of the wrong. Such an award will usually be followed by an award of costs.

Constantine v Imperial Hotels Ltd [1944]

The plaintiff, a famous West Indian cricketer, was unreasonably refused entry to the defendant's hotel. However, the plaintiff did not suffer any actual damage as a result.
Held: The plaintiff was awarded five guineas in nominal damages as a result of the unlawful discrimination. *Constantine v Imperial Hotels Ltd* [1944] 1 K.B. 693.

4. Contemptuous Damages

Key Principle: Such damages are awarded to a plaintiff who is legally entitled to succeed, but the court wishes to mark its displeasure towards the plaintiff's claim which might be seen as frivolous or vexatious. The award is usually represented by the "smallest coin of the realm". An award of costs may not follow an award of contemptuous damages.

Grobbelaar v News Group Newspapers Ltd [2002]

The plaintiff was a famous professional footballer. The defendant published a series of articles alleging that the plaintiff had dishonestly taken bribes, had fixed or attempted to fix the result of games of football in which he had played and that he had taken bribes with a view to fixing the result of games in which he would be playing in. The allegations were based on video recordings made of the plaintiff in conversation with another individual where he discussed receiving such payments and discussed fixing the results in games. The plaintiff argued that he had never thrown football games for money and that the recorded conversations were just a ploy by the plaintiff to discover who was behind the match-fixing attempt. In action for defamation, the plaintiff was awarded damages of £85,000 by a jury. The defendant appealed the verdict of the jury as perverse and the award was successfully overturned by the Court of Appeal. The plaintiff appealed to the House of Lords.

Held: While the defendant had technically defamed the plaintiff, the House of Lords reinstated the jury's original verdict in favour of the plaintiff but reduced the award of damages to £1. While the defendant had not proven that the plaintiff had thrown games of football, other evidence showed that he was guilty of behavior which no honest or decent professional footballer should have been guilty of. *Grobbelaar v News Group Newspapers Ltd* [2002] U.K.H.L. 40.

5. Exemplary/Punitive Damages

Key Principle: Such damages are generally awarded where the conduct of the defendant or the wrong committed by him or her attracts the strong disapproval of the courts. Such damages are awarded generally, for example, in circumstances where there is oppressive, arbitrary or unconstitutional conduct by servants of the government or in circumstances where the defendant's conduct was calculated to make a profit in excess of the compensation that would be ordinarily recoverable by the plaintiff.

Shortt v The Commissioner of the Garda & the AG [2007]

The plaintiff was the victim of a shocking abuse of power by members of the Gardaí. The plaintiff was falsely accused and charged with allowing his licensed premises to be used for the sale of drugs. To compound matters, the Gardaí committed perjury during his prosecution. As a result, the plaintiff wrongly spent a number of years in jail.

Held: The Supreme Court awarded the plaintiff a record €1 million in exemplary damages. Murray C.J. pointed out that such damages were necessary given the serious nature of the abuse in this case and the fact that the award of punitive/exemplary damages would act as a deterrent effect to the arrogant use or abuse of power. *Shortt v The Commissioner of the Garda & the AG* [2007] I.E.S.C. 9.

Crofter Properties Ltd v Genport Ltd [2005]

An action was brought by a corporation—in this case a hotel—alleging that the business had been defamed by the defendant. A number of calls had been made by the secretary of the defendant on his behalf to a police unit in England. These phone calls alleged that the individual and his brother were using the hotel to launder money for the IRA.

Held: The High Court awarded €250,000 in exemplary damages given the malicious and deliberate nature of the calls. This award was reduced on appeal by the Supreme Court. *Crofter Properties Ltd v Genport Ltd* [2005] I.E.H.C. 94.

INDEX